HOW WE ALMOST GAVE THE TORIES THE BOOT

HOW WE ALMOST GAVE THE TORIES
THE BOOT

(the inside story
behind the coalition)

a memoir by Brian Topp

LORIMER

james lorimer & company ltd., publishers
toronto

James Lorimer & Company Ltd., Publishers acknowledge the support of the Ontario Arts Council. We acknowledge the support of the Government of Canada through the Book Publishing Industry Development Program (BPIDP) for our publishing activities. We acknowledge the support of the Canada Council for the Arts for our publishing program. We acknowledge the support of the Government of Ontario through the Ontario Media Development Corporation's Ontario Book Initiative.

Portions of this book originally appeared in serialized form in the "politics" section of the Toronto *Globe and Mail's* online edition: www.globeandmail.com/politics

 Canada Council   Conseil des Arts
for the Arts   du Canada

 ONTARIO ARTS COUNCIL
CONSEIL DES ARTS DE L'ONTARIO

Design: Meghan Collins
Cover illustration: istockphoto.com
Library and Archives Canada Cataloguing in Publication
Topp, Brian, 1960-
How we almost gave the Tories the boot : the inside story behind the coalition / Brian Topp.
ISBN 978-1-55277-502-8
1. Topp, Brian, 1960-. 2. Coalitions—Canada. 3. Coalition governments—Canada. 4. Canada—Politics and government—2006-.
I. Title.
FC640.T66 2010   971.07'3092   C2010-900203-2
James Lorimer & Company Ltd., Publishers
317 Adelaide Street West, Suite 1002
Toronto, Ontario
M5V 1P9
www.lorimer.ca

Printed in Canada

"Never mind the manoeuvres,
always go straight at 'em."

—Lord Nelson, as quoted by Patrick O'Brian

Contents

Foreword

by the Honourable Roy Romanow, PC, OC, QC, SOM

Premier of Saskatchewan, 1991-2001

THIS BOOK ABOUT A MULTI-PARTY AGREEMENT to create a national coalition government is of substantial interest to me, both as a Canadian citizen and as the former premier of Saskatchewan who participated in the creation of a provincial coalition government.

My objective in this foreword is to set the scene, by briefly explaining the factors that led to that provincial coalition government. I'll also offer a few comments on the legitimacy of properly constituted coalition governments, the legitimacy of the tripartite agreement for a national coalition government that is the subject of this book, and the current and future value of this book itself.

My experience with a coalition government is rooted in the results of Saskatchewan's general election in the fall of 1999, when no political party had enough members to form a majority government, but my party had the most members.

My challenge was to find a way to govern effectively in what was clearly a highly politicized and partisan legislature. Knowing the actors and their stated positions, my sense was that compromise, especially by the reinvigorated official Opposition, was highly improbable. Political positioning, exaggerated oratory, and strategic partisan tactics, always a part of legislative debate, would now characterize every major decision taken by any of the political parties.

In this context, I feared that my government's ambitious agenda since 1991, namely fiscal sustainability, economic development, and reforms in various policy fields, but especially in the health-care field, would be severely compromised or derailed.

It was with that in mind that I began to contemplate a coalition government as an alternative way to continue to govern and provide stability and continuity for at least two years. The hurdles to forming a coalition government were many and high.

Several questions emerged that needed answers. Would my own caucus and political party agree? Would the public perceive this development as a crass political manoeuvre to thwart its voting intentions? Could we agree upon a four-year agenda that closely followed the objectives of the previous eight years? Could we maintain cabinet solidarity? Would constitutional conventions, such as the premier's prerogative to select cabinet, be respected?

To get answers to some of those questions, a meeting was held with the leader of the Liberal party. Somewhat surprisingly, general agreement on the principle of a coalition government was quickly reached, but subject to satisfactory conclusions about the important details and principles. One paramount and shared principle was that both political parties would remain independent entities.

A working committee of senior officials was established to tackle the important principles and details associated with this venture. Thus, Brian Topp, a close advisor to me, joined a tightly knit team of legal, constitutional, and political experts to negotiate those principles and details. Written agreements between the party leaders and their respective political parties were to be executed and released to the public for its consideration. Constitutional principles and customs were to be confirmed and allocation of cabinet positions and government duties assigned. Like most important matters, the negotiations were difficult and did not always end well on all issues. But, in the end, core public-policy purposes and fundamental constitutional principles were identified and documented. This was done to enable the public to judge our actions.

As may be expected, our initiative was greeted with considerable skepticism and criticism. The criticism hinged on the following points: that we had not received an electoral mandate to engage in this enterprise; that the voters had not elected a coalition government; and that the agreement violated the foundations of parliamentary democracy.

It is in relation to that last point of criticism that this book is extremely important, because it assists us in understanding the true nature of parliamentary democracy—whether or not there is a majority, minority, or coalition government. Brian Topp describes in a clear and compelling manner what actually transpired "behind the curtains" in Ottawa in late 2008 when a federal coalition government was almost established. The narrative is invaluable because it "parts the curtains" and instructs us on how many parliamentary agreements are actually made in this manner. Most important, however, this book helps us to understand the fundamental constitutional principles at play when coalition governments are contemplated and established.

In simple terms, the fundamental rule is this: the party leader who can command the support of a majority of the elected members, no matter how that majority is comprised and no matter how many political parties are involved in comprising that coalition, will become the first minister and possess the legal and moral authority to appoint members of his or her government. This is one of the fundamental principles on which the legitimacy of governmental authority rests in our constitutional system.

Thus, Prime Minister Stephen Harper was simply wrong in 2008 and irresponsible in his arguments when, in attacking the embryonic coalition, he claimed the right to stay in power simply because his own political party held the most seats. It proved to be an extremely effective political argument that eventually led to the abandonment of the signed coalition agreement. But it was blind to the fundamental constitutional underpinnings of our parliamentary democracy and, if pursued in the future, might lead to problems in Parliament and in the broader political system.

Without a definite and clear understanding of, and commitment to, the principle that each elected legislator has the constitutional right to support the party or parties of his or her choice, Canadians risk descending into constitutional and political crisis or chaos. This could happen either when elections do not give a single party the majority of seats, or when a loss of confidence by a government leads a governor general or lieutenant-governor to call on Opposition parties to see if they can obtain the requisite degree of support among elected legislators to form a government.

The Canadian parliamentary system allows individual elected members to express their confidence in governments, and it allows political parties to enter into agreements on, among other things, the precise composition of the cabinet.

I am not suggesting that the proposed coalition agreement of 2008 and the negotiations that led to it were necessarily a promising basis for the formation of an effective new government in Canada. After all, there is no guarantee that the coalition government that was envisioned would have identified the proper remedies, selected the right cabinet members, and dealt with issues efficiently and effectively. Those are things that we shall never know, because the coalition did not materialize.

What I am suggesting is that proper process is exactly what our constitution and its conventions demand in forming a government in all instances, including when the election results do not provide a single party with enough seats to form a majority government or when a government loses the confidence of the House of Commons or a provincial legislature.

In my estimation, the proper process was followed in 2008, and the coalition agreement was neither undemocratic nor underhanded. The agreement was the result of the fact that Prime Minister Harper and his government had lost the confidence of members of the Opposition parties on a fundamental matter of public policy. When such an event occurs, Canadians are extremely fortunate that our parliamentary system has the constitutional option of a coalition government, with another leader and another agenda, to advance the public good. This is far better than frequent elections that might undermine society's faith in our democratic processes and contribute to continuous and futile bickering in Parliament when decisive action is required.

This book describes a very important moment in Canadian history, a time when duly elected Opposition parties concluded that the public interest would be better served by a coalition government.

This book also provides important insights regarding procedural and political facts related to those negotiations and the resulting agreement, and does so in an elegant and engaging manner.

If I may be permitted a personal note, I am particularly pleased to acknowledge the key role played in these events by the Honourable Allan Blakeney, my predecessor as leader of the Saskatchewan New Democratic Party. I worked in close partnership with Mr. Blakeney as his deputy during his memorable term as premier of Saskatchewan. It is a real pleasure to read about the important role he played in this attempt to bring Canada better government. This book demonstrates the intelligence and principles of a committed Canadian, and thus is instructive. Canadians were fortunate that he was there to provide his wise counsel.

Above all, however, this book reminds us of the importance of our parliamentary system and the principles upon which it stands. When we forget them, ignore them, or, worse yet, denigrate and disparage them, we run the risk of fostering potentially destructive political instability.

Preface

"Why do we want to give away our playbook?"

That was a good question, put to me by one of the key players in the events I'm about to describe, after reading an earlier draft of this book.

Why? For several good reasons, I think.

First, because Canadians have the right to know what those of us who tried to replace Stephen Harper's government with a better one thought we were doing. We helped provoke a first-class political and constitutional crisis. How? Why? To what end?

Second, because it is never wise in politics to allow opponents to have the last word. Our attempt, in the fall of 2008, to give Prime Minister Stephen Harper's government "the boot" and to replace it with a new and better government drew withering criticism which, as I will show, we were unable to answer effectively at the time. In a small way, now that the dust has settled, telling this side of the story is a chance to balance the books.

And third, because some important lessons were learned that should be made explicit before anything like this is tried again. The majority in the 2008 Parliament attempted a legitimate and appropriate replacement of a ministry, entirely in keeping with the rules and precedents of our parliamentary system of government. But we made a number of important mistakes that should not be repeated. A good place to start, as we shall see, would be to take greater care to ensure that all parties to a potential new government are really committed to the project.

I helped lead one of the negotiating teams involved in these events. Over three days, we put together the first formal parliamentary coalition Canada has seen since 1917, with the goal of replacing the minority Harper government with a new, better, progressive government in command of a stable majority in the House of Commons.

As Lord Nelson, via Patrick O'Brian, might say, we went straight at 'em.

These events created an unusually interesting episode in the history of our Canadian Parliament, I think. They both served as a reminder of the latent power of our elected institutions and, unfortunately, ultimately provided another step in Parliament's marginalization.

There were many other players on the NDP, Conservative, Liberal, and Bloc teams. I hope they tell their stories too—about this episode and about this interesting period of our parliamentary history.

Much of what really happens in our political system is hidden these days. First-person political memoirs are a partial antidote to this. There are too few of these in Canada (*Gentlemen, Players and Politicians* by Dalton Camp is the hands-down best ever written in English Canada, in my view). But political memoirs must not pose as objective or complete. Certainly this book is not. It's what one person saw. I tell you this to warn you that I haven't tried to write a comprehensive or definitive history of the 2008 coalition episode. That is work for a historian. Good luck! I promise to buy your book.

I began pulling my notes together a few months after we concluded the coalition agreement. It was a sobering experience in how fleeting memory is. I was far too busy during those days to keep a diary, but I did keep one during the 2008 federal election campaign immediately preceding, when much of our thinking about this project took place. I had a notebook in which I scribbled working notes and interesting statements during the coalition negotiations. And I sent and received a tidal wave of e-mails by BlackBerry before, during, and after the talks. They were the channel through which much of this work was done. I'm going to weave some of this material into the pages that follow.

Where people are directly quoted during meetings in what follows, I am relying on verbatim notes I took at the time. The e-mails are verbatim with some light editing to correct the vagaries of correspondence typed with thumbs on small keyboards.

In a nutshell, here is what happened from our perspective.

During the 2004, 2006, and 2008 federal election campaigns, federal NDP leader Jack Layton directed his campaign team to create study groups to consider and make recommendations about his options in Parliament post-campaign. Terry Grier ably chaired this effort in 2004. I co-ordinated it in 2006 and 2008.

Layton piloted his approach to parliamentary accords during the 2004–2006 Martin minority, producing the 2005 NDP budget that served Canada well.

After the 2008 election, our party approached the Liberal Party of Canada and gently floated the idea of replacing the minority Conservative government with a formal Liberal–NDP coalition. This suggestion was politely rebuffed.

Later that fall, Prime Minister Stephen Harper made a crucial parliamentary mistake, which opened the door to the renewal of this project—and quick agreement on an accord between the NDP and the Liberals, supported by the Bloc Québécois.

Mr. Harper's skilful, if democratically dubious, parliamentary manoeuvring then closed the very brief window of opportunity the resulting coalition had. The Liberal caucus took their cue from Mr. Harper and buried the coalition by replacing Stéphane Dion with a small "c" conservative leader, Michael Ignatieff.

In January 2009, Mr. Ignatieff formally reneged on his own signature and those of his caucus, repudiating the coalition accords and entering into a parliamentary ceasefire with Mr. Harper that was more to Mr. Ignatieff's liking.

To be fair to Mr. Ignatieff, he was pursuing a coherent objective in doing these things. He wanted to solidify his leadership of the Liberal Party, recharge its financial, organizational, and intellectual batteries, and then challenge the Harper government the traditional way—in a spring or fall 2009 federal election.

This strategy foundered because it required the co-operation of both the NDP and the Bloc Québécois, which Mr. Ignatieff did not secure. The result, at least in the short term, was damaging to Mr. Ignatieff's party and helpful to both the Conservative government and to the New Democrats.

So we didn't kick out the Harper Conservative government and replace it with something better, as we had set out to do. But we did make some progress. Using their brief moment of common purpose with the Liberals and the Bloc, Jack Layton and the New Democrats forced the Conservatives to react to the economic crisis gripping our country with a package of economic measures they adamantly opposed and would never otherwise have introduced. In addition, the Conservative attempt to reintroduce big money to federal politics was withdrawn.

Further, the Liberal and New Democratic bargaining teams created a prototype of a form of government that is likely to be a part of Canada's future.

For good or ill, a large majority of Quebec's seats in Parliament are now occupied by a Parnellite ethnic nationalist party—the Bloc Québécois. As I write, their separatist agenda is moribund. But the perversity of our first-past-the-post electoral system seems to leave them secure in most of their seats (that said, a by-election on November 9, 2009, flipped one of the Bloc's rural seats to the Conservatives. There are no certainties in politics). Therefore, as was the case in Britain for much of the nineteenth century, when most Irish seats in the British Parliament were occupied by a similar formation, the lock that Quebec's separatist minority seems to have on much of that province's federal parliamentary delegation makes it hard to see how any of the national Canadian parties, as currently configured, can obtain a ruling majority by themselves for very long.

Canada has in any event more fully become the multi-party democracy we have been for almost a hundred years—like most Western democracies. This is why most Western democracies are governed by stable coalition governments.

The basic issues of such governments—questions of how they should be structured and what is their common policy agenda—were discussed in the last weeks of 2008. That was useful groundwork, since I suspect this is not the last time a federal party (whether the New Democrats or another party) will consider serving the country in partnership in this way.

A few thanks are in order.

I'm grateful to NDP leader Jack Layton for giving me the opportunity to be a part of these events and for many other courtesies and opportunities. I'm also grateful to my colleagues Anne McGrath and Sue Milling for their partnership during this work, and to Premier Allan Blakeney, Premier Roy Romanow, and former federal NDP leader Ed Broadbent for their guidance and wisdom during these events.

Bill Knight, George Nakitsas, and Robin Sears were co-architects of what is still our tribe's best run so far at winning federal office. They have been thoughtful, helpful counsellors to their successors since then (one of the most difficult things to do in politics), including during the work described in this book.

Rick Boychuk asked some of the tough questions raised by an earlier draft—to its benefit—and was most helpful to this project in many other ways.

A portion of what follows was serialized at www.globeandmail.com in December 2009, on its "politics" pages. That serial drew over 50,000 hits, which apparently isn't bad as these things go. In an era of monolithically conservative media in English Canada, *The Globe and Mail* has opened its Internet presence wide to voices from many perspectives. It is almost unique in doing so. As part of that effort, the editors of *The Globe and Mail* have bravely given me a regular spot in their online space, for which I am thankful.

I have had the privilege of working for outstanding elected presidents and councils at ACTRA Toronto, my employer. Our union blends commitment to protecting performers with relentless advocacy of arts-friendly and film-friendly public policy. ACTRA also supports the political process by letting its people participate in it, when the press of our work permits. Presidents Richard Hardacre, Karl Pruner, and Heather Allin have been more than generous in granting me leaves of unpredictable length to work on the issues I will describe in this book. I'm very proud of the place and of the folks I work for.

Kim Hume proofread this manuscript with her usual meticulous care.

Many thanks to Jim Lorimer, Diane Young, Pat Kennedy, Kerry Cathers and the team at Lorimer for taking on this project and turning it into a book. I'm quite proud that this work will join the impressive roster of titles published by Jim and his colleagues. Remaining errors are my own.

Most of all, I'm thankful to my wife, Rebecca, and our ever-taller sons Simon and Alex for putting up with my political work. The minority Parliaments of the first decade of the twenty-first century gave those involved in Canadian federal politics quite a ride. It's nice to be home.

—Toronto, November 2009

Part One
Prologue

Prologue

PERHAPS A GOOD PLACE TO BEGIN is with a brief sketch of how I came to be involved in these events.

I was born and raised in Montreal.

My family on the Topp side moved from a hamlet in Aberdeenshire, Scotland to the big city of Granby, Quebec in the 1870s to work in the tobacco and rubber mills there. The Lamère, Méthot, Marchildon, and Prévost families on my mother's side have roots in and around Trois-Rivières and Quebec City going back to the foundation of New France.

In the mid-1980s, I discovered that an undergraduate history degree from McGill University (an excellent thing in every other way) did not instantly lead in my case to fabulous and glamorous employment at the salary to which my fellow graduates and I were entitled. So, I was living in a $300-a-month tenement apartment over some stores on the corner of Ontario and Papineau Streets in east-end Montreal.

It was a warm and fascinating community, solidly Québécois working class at the time. Many neighbours were employed at the enormous tobacco factory down the street.

One of the first-floor businesses on our block was an ancient grocery store decorated with a gigantic, faded, elaborately framed painting of John A. Macdonald, which had hung in its place for at least a hundred years—not a typical store decoration in that part of town.

Every morning, six or seven days a week, I walked to work at a small typesetting and graphic-design studio nestled among the rooming houses on St. Hubert Street, a bit closer to downtown.

I had launched that enterprise (generally operating with three to five employees, collectively scratching out a living on perhaps $250,000 in total corporate income in a good year) to try to finance a small, amateurish city news and culture magazine, which had quickly folded. The magazine came and went in eighteen months, but its debts stayed with me for many years, slowly paid off via the typesetting and design firm.

We called our little enterprise "Studio Apostrophe" to gently thumb our noses at our province's language laws—absolutely necessary and correct laws, to be clear—that had removed English-language apostrophes from store signs across Montreal (thus "Eaton's" had become "Eaton"). We put an apostrophe back up. Our francophone clients liked the name because it made them think of poetry. Our anglophone clients mostly got the joke.

Over the years, off and on, we cornered much of the market for typesetting among Montreal's progressive, union, student, small-press tabloid, and gay press. The money wasn't great (to indulge in a laugh-out-loud understatement) but the clients and the neighbourhood were consistently bohemian, creative, multicultural, and interesting. There was rarely a dull day during the high noon of Studio Apostrophe.

In 1984, NDP leader Ed Broadbent initiated a four-year campaign to restart his party in Quebec, ably assisted by his senior staff team, including (in various roles) George Nakitsas, Bill Knight, and Robin Sears. Several of my school friends signed up as NDP organizers or newly signed-up party activists. They appeared at our typesetting shop to set up posters and pamphlets. I usually let them do these for nominal fees or for free, as circumstances seemed to warrant.

I found their enthusiasm infectious. And I found what I was reading in those pamphlets increasingly persuasive.

One of our typesetting clients, auto-consumer advocate Phil Edmonston, was recruited by Broadbent's team to run for the NDP in the 1988 federal election. At his request, I chaired that campaign and the subsequent, victorious by-election campaign that sent Edmonston to Parliament as the NDP's first elected Quebec MP. He offered me a job, and so, in December 1989, I handed Studio Apostrophe over to its employees and moved to Ottawa.

In 1992, I went to work at NDP Research as a researcher and writer.

In 1993, I accepted an irresistible offer to become director of research in the Department of Executive Council of the government of Saskatchewan, led by Premier Roy Romanow.

In 1995, I was promoted to deputy chief of staff in that office. In this role I handled a number of files, including our government's legislative business office (which oversaw the government's business in the legislature as the support arm to the government house leader); the premier's speechwriting shop; our media-services unit; oversight of our communications consulting unit; our research and question period unit; government polling; and—the best part—a mandate to offer political and communications advice to the premier when he wanted it.

As was helpfully pointed out to me many times by many of my colleagues at the Saskatchewan legislature, I was completely unqualified for any of these roles. I was a sometimes arrogant thirty-four-year-old Quebecer, completely new to the province and its legislature, on my first senior political job (from some perspectives my first real job of any kind), who was offering advice to a veteran premier who had been a master of Saskatchewan politics and government for three decades.

The Goddess knows why they put me there.

But what wonderful fun it all was. I went to work eagerly, in the early years of that gig starting at 5:30 a.m. (later amended to a more civilized 7:00 a.m.) and often working long into the night. There was always something new or remarkable to do.

We travelled all around the world.

I sat in on some high-stakes inter-provincial and federal-provincial meetings, including a couple of extremely interesting evenings at 24 Sussex Drive, one of which I will describe below.

Much rubbery lemon chicken was eaten at the Saskatoon cabinet office and at Premier Romanow's Regina condo, while reviewing events of the day, and holding the occasional informal political meeting.

For example, I once attended an evening discussion between Premier Romanow and a friend of his, a senior Saskatchewan federal Liberal. Premier Romanow's friend tried to persuade Mr. Romanow to call Jean Chrétien right away to tell him that it was time to retire and make way for Finance Minister Paul Martin. Premier Romanow declined to make this call. It seemed odd to me that federal Liberals were trying to use leaders from other parties as instruments in their civil war.

Very early on in this job, I understood that an important part of it involved talking carefully with the Opposition parties.

Elected and political staff in different political parties compete ferociously in public, but can work together productively and cooperatively off-camera, and often get along well after hours. This was certainly true in the Saskatchewan legislature, which faithfully reflects the warm, cooperative culture of the people it serves. Those working at the legislature in Saskatchewan are generally friendly, approachable, and get along, while reserving a streak of unblinking ruthlessness for occasions that require it.

I spent a lot of time chatting with the Conservative and Liberal political staffs. I came to admire the Tory political team, led by chief-of-staff Reg Downs, as they slowly recovered and rebuilt from the catastrophic inheritance left to them by former premier Grant Devine. The same core Tory political staff remained in place from 1991 until they finally won. They are sitting in our former offices as I write, having finally pulled off what seemed like an impossible political task, electing a new Conservative government under Premier Brad Wall, once one of Mr. Devine's political aides. The NDP at every level has lessons to learn from the Saskatchewan Conservatives—beginning with their cheerful, unbending determination to succeed. Let's be like that.

Getting to know the Opposition paid dividends. After talking to them enough, it became possible to predict their moves—provided that you also read everything they read, listened to everything they listened to, and kept an eye on the interest groups they were trying to play with. By doing this, our team became adept at anticipating the Opposition's plans and preparing for them. At our best, the game in our "hot room" behind the government side of the legislature during question period wasn't to predict Opposition questions, but to predict the order in which they would be asked. Sometimes we got them bang on. Then, having anticipated them, our cabinet was ready for them, which might mean another no-news day for the Opposition.

In 1997, I took a leave of absence from the government of Saskatchewan and went to Ottawa to manage the war room of the federal NDP's 1997 election campaign. Federal leader Alexa McDonough fought a spirited and well-targeted campaign, designed by national campaign director David Woodbury and McDonough's chief of staff Dan O'Connor. We won twenty-one members of Parliament and a return to party status. I shared the campaign team's joyous relief and deep gratitude to Alexa McDonough for leading our party back from its less encouraging 1993 showing. I also viewed the campaign as a training exercise. I returned to my job in Regina with the next Saskatchewan provincial election on my mind.

It was going to be a tough campaign.

All across the great plains in the United States and Canada there stand ghost towns, abandoned rail lines, and other decaying infrastructure slowly being ploughed under by ever-larger farm operations. Dry-land grain cultivation is a tough business in many ways. Its economics at the end of the twentieth century mitigated against compact family farms and drove the industry towards high-volume, low-margin corporate operations.

These realities were playing themselves out in rural Saskatchewan. There were perhaps fifty thousand farms in Saskatchewan when I worked there. A senior official in our agriculture department once told me that there was a market that would maintain perhaps five thousand real operations—gigantic, capital-intensive, and tended by a much smaller rural population.

The province's rural infrastructure—the schools, hospitals, rail net, road, and grain-handling system—was being adjusted to deal with this reality. The old underpinnings of rural life—the co-operatives, credit unions, and pools—were "adjusting" as well. People in the farm economy knew better than anyone what was happening. They were making it happen. They were voting for it at pool and co-op meetings. They were financing much of it. But they didn't have to like it.

They also didn't have to like a provincial NDP government that knew it could not immediately act on their pleas to eliminate education taxes, or to finance cash payments to offset grain subsidies paid by national governments to competitors in other countries, or to do something—anything—about disastrously low agricultural commodity prices, or to instantly fix thousands of miles of fragile rural roads that were being pounded to dust and mud by the new monster grain trucks that were replacing short-line rail lines. Our campaign failed to be persuasive on these issues.

So, in the 1999 Saskatchewan provincial election—sweetened by a tactically opportunistic and strategically mindless nurses' strike, timed by that union's leaders to politically blackmail our government and which we did not handle well—rural voters defeated almost every rural New Democrat in the legislature.

Urban voters remained faithful to Premier Romanow.

We found ourselves on election night with a legislature composed of 29 New Democrats, 25 Conservatives, and 4 Liberals (one of whom would have his election invalidated, losing his seat to the Conservatives in a subsequent by-election).

Given the likely need to supply a Speaker, we had lost our majority.

These results were clear by 9:00 p.m. on election night. By 10:30 p.m., Premier Romanow and deputy premier Dwain Lingenfelter had agreed on what needed to be done. Liberal leader Jim Melenchuk was called that evening and was offered cabinet seats in a new coalition government. He agreed to explore the idea. Premier Romanow therefore put together a working group to advise him as he set about crafting a new coalition government. As part of its work, he dispatched me to go and have a few words with Dr. Melenchuk's staff team.

My first meeting with the Liberal staff was disheartening. The principal thing on their minds was an expectation that an advertising firm that had worked on the Liberal campaign would get a fitting share of government business. My duty was to ensure no false hopes were raised about this, while probing to see how interested they were in working with us—and on what terms.

What became clear was that Dr. Melenchuk and his caucus colleagues liked and admired Premier Romanow, disliked the stone-faced members of the Conservative caucus (who were, foolishly, ignoring them), and were very interested indeed in discussing an arrangement. Having established this and having very roughly outlined the shape of an accord, we reported back to our principals, who then met over a series of days and concluded an agreement. In October 1999, only a few days after the election, Romanow and Melenchuk announced their coalition.

The NDP–Liberal Saskatchewan government went on to serve the province ably for four years. It was, I submit, an excellent template for how such a government could be conducted, although our coalition partner made some important mistakes, which I'll discuss below.

Once the coalition was safely in place and in light of the underlying election result, I fired myself, moved back east, took up a job in the credit-union system and then with ACTRA, and vowed that I was going to stay out of politics.

In the summer of 2002, my Toronto city councillor, David Miller, got in touch with me through a mutual friend. Over a cup of coffee, he outlined his plan to run for mayor and asked me if I might like to sit in on his election planning committee to offer any advice I might have. I liked him, and I liked the chutzpah of his campaign. He had perhaps 5-per-cent name recognition among voters at the time. I decided to bend my "out of politics" rule and agreed to sit in on his committee. In a campaign directed by Conservative *éminence grise* John Laschinger, Miller went on to win an inspiring and remarkable victory. And he launched a sorely needed, broad-front, and increasingly successful effort to renew and rejuvenate Toronto, Canada's much abused, disgracefully exploited, and (at that time) increasingly threadbare leading city.

(As an aside, the bitter public-sector strike that preceded Mayor Miller's announcement in the fall of 2009 that he would not run for a third term had a familiar ring to veterans of NDP governments. Public-sector bargaining is one of the progressive left's proudest achievements in Canada. It is also perhaps our greatest gift to the political right, who lie in wait for it to destroy our governments, and then often find ways to outlaw it when they rule.)

Some of our Miller campaign committee meetings were filmed by Andrew Munger, a documentary filmmaker. In late 2003, newly elected federal NDP leader Jack Layton watched the result, *Campaign: The Making of a Candidate,* caught my name and a glimpse of me saying a few words, connected me to the Saskatchewan NDP team, and gave me a call.

Layton had been elected federal leader with the support of Ed Broadbent and many others whom I respect a great deal, as well as with the support of leading voices on the oppositional left of our party. Now he seemed interested in building a "big tent" team that also included some people with experience in NDP governments.

Mr. Layton is a persuasive man. In due course I agreed to apply for a leave from work and to serve again as manager of the NDP war room during the 2004 federal election campaign.

On some measures we did well, doubling the NDP's vote to more than two million (2,127,403 to be precise, compared to 1,093,868 in 2000). But the 19-seat harvest (compared to 13 in 2000) was extremely disappointing.

I was critical of some elements of our campaign. It seemed to me we had failed to focus on a single, clear opponent. We had run on a grab bag of themes and issues. Our team had developed a list of "eight priorities," which were largely ignored throughout the election. We had concurrently drafted a wildly unhelpful policy platform, including a commitment to introducing inheritance taxes which was repudiated in mid-campaign. Our ground-game dissipated our resources, resulting in the loss of too many close ridings. Our senior campaign leadership had exhausted itself discussing all of this and didn't seem to work well together.

As fit punishment for making these points, I was invited to try to do better as co-chair of the federal NDP's election planning committee and as national campaign director for the next campaign. Keen to improve our results, I agreed to do this.

For good or ill, my campaign colleagues and I tried to address the lacunae revealed in our 2004 campaign. We focused our negative messaging, tried to design a policy offer that hung together better, and were more disciplined in our allocation of resources on the ground. I also tried to give our central campaign team a taste of the Douglas–Blakeney–Romanow staff system, which promotes discussion but is not tolerant of dysfunction.

In the 2006 federal election campaign, our party increased its vote (to 2,589,597 votes, each one beautiful), and won 29 seats.

Layton invited me to remain in place and—still not satisfied with the seat number—I agreed to do so. For the most part, the rest of our campaign team also remained in place, and we set to work shortly after the 2006 campaign to plan the next one.

The bright young team Layton had recruited to Ottawa now came into their own. They internalized the "fixes" implemented in 2006—a clear target, a disciplined message, a tight ground game, the basic elements of teamwork—and built on them with a sparkling leader's tour, a fresh new approach to our paid media, and many other improvements.

We still made heartbreaking mistakes, such as the self-inflicted wound of grotesquely inappropriate candidacies in a handful of ridings, which were lovingly covered in the media for endless days during the campaign in lieu of what we were actually trying to say. I would like to think we learned from this elementary mistake, for which I must take responsibility, with a post-election reform that tightened up future nominations. Aspirants to our colours must now be pre-approved by our national party before they can even run for nominations.

Still, some things worked.

In the 2008 federal election, we held our vote (2,515,561, and on a notably low overall turnout, but who's counting?), and won 37 seats, the second-best result in the federal NDP's history in another minority Parliament.

So then, things got interesting.

Let's back up a bit.

In early 2004, at about the same time he was talking to me about joining his first federal campaign, Layton had directed that a low-profile working committee be formed to think about his options after his first federal election. Layton planned an extremely ambitious campaign in 2004, running to win in 150 ridings. He hoped to double or triple the NDP vote, in a perfect world to emerge from the election as the largest party, and then to negotiate some sort of arrangement with other parties in Parliament to govern the country.

It was nothing if not ambitious, and exactly what the party was looking for when it elected him federal leader.

Layton's mentor and friend Terry Grier was tapped to co-ordinate that committee, which didn't really have a name. "Scenarios committee" is one way to think about it. Grier's committee met steadily through early 2004, eventually producing a carefully considered package with a strategy note and a number of appendices. In this material, Grier and his colleagues considered all the possible permutations—NDP minority, Tory minority, Liberal minority, NDP in balance-of-power position, NDP and Bloc both in balance-of-power positions, etc.—and made recommendations on how Layton and his caucus colleagues might play their cards.

The Grier committee took a look at the "accord" arrangements negotiated between Bob Rae and David Peterson in 1985, as well as at various coalition agreements in other countries, and appended some of the working documents from these.

The basic message to the leader was something he had a mind to listen to: use whatever power you earn in the election to get as much done as possible in the next Parliament.

The perversities of Canada's electoral system played out in the June 28, 2004, election, which doubled the NDP vote but gave us only those 19 seats—not quite enough to hold the balance of power in the newly elected minority Parliament.

Nonetheless, Layton gave it a try. Through a number of indirect channels and then directly during a flight to a meeting, Layton suggested to Prime Minister Martin that some sort of arrangement be negotiated between the NDP and the Liberals, trading support in the house for progress on issues the NDP wanted emphasized.

Prime Minister Martin scoffed at this offer, telling Layton airily that the NDP had too few seats for Layton to be worth talking to. Presumably Martin was confident that he would be able to keep his government in office with the support of Opposition leader Stephen Harper or Bloc Québécois leader Gilles Duceppe.

But unlike Mr. Martin, we had a pretty good idea of what was on the minds of the Tories and the Bloc Québécois. They were working on a very different scenario.

In a series of meetings that summer of 2004, first bilaterally, between Stephen Harper and Gilles Duceppe, and then in three-party talks, the Opposition parties met to talk about what to do about Mr. Martin and his apparent determination to govern as if he had a majority.

Harper and Duceppe, later joined by Layton, sketched out a plan to send the minority Liberal government a message that it was going to have to govern in consultation with the Opposition parties. To that end, a package of amendments to the government's upcoming Throne Speech was developed. The NDP contributed a number of ideas to this package, focused on parliamentary reform.

On September 9, 2004, the three leaders sent the following letter to Governor General Adrienne Clarkson:

Excellency,

As leaders of the Opposition parties, we are well aware that, given the Liberal minority government, you could be asked by the Prime Minister to dissolve the 38th Parliament at any time should the House of Commons fail to support some part of the government's program.

We respectfully point out that the Opposition parties, who together constitute a majority in the house, have been in close consultation. We believe that, should a request for dissolution arise this should give you cause, as constitutional practice has determined, to consult the Opposition leaders and consider all of your options before exercising your constitutional authority.

Your attention to this matter is appreciated.

Sincerely,

Hon. Stephen Harper, PC, MP
Leader of the Opposition
Leader of the Conservative Party of Canada

Gilles Duceppe, MP
Leader of the Bloc Québécois

Jack Layton, MP
Leader of the New Democratic Party

The meaning of this letter is perfectly plain. In the event that Mr. Martin's government was defeated in a confidence vote, the three leaders were asking the governor general to consider turning to the Opposition for a new government in lieu of giving Prime Minister Martin a dissolution. Mr. Harper, Mr. Duceppe, and Mr. Layton were thus jointly arguing that the governor general was duty bound to take account not only of the views of the prime minister, but also of the views of the majority of the House of Commons in those circumstances.

In his book, *Speaking Out Louder*, Layton relates what happened next:

> *Gilles Duceppe wanted all the changes we had agreed upon to be put forward in an amendment to the Speech from the Throne. As the most experienced Opposition leader, he clearly wanted to move into the driver's seat, and successfully did so for the first couple of meetings. Forcing the Liberals to accept our recommendations as an amendment to the Speech from the Throne amounted to a game of parliamentary "chicken." If the government refused, Mr. Duceppe pointed out, the three parties had enough votes to ensure its defeat.*
>
> *Waiting outside Mr. Harper's office for our meeting to begin, I asked Mr. Duceppe what he thought would happen if the prime minister refused to accept such an ultimatum. He replied that a government defeat so soon after a general election meant the Governor General would have to turn "to one of us" to form a government. We both knew that meant Stephen Harper and his Conservatives. I asked Mr. Duceppe if he could accept such an eventuality. He was not only clear that he could, but he would.*

Confronted with this blunt talk, and in these circumstances, Layton concluded he and our party had no obvious interest in making Stephen Harper prime minister. He therefore withdrew from the three-party group. No longer in control of the entire Opposition bench, the two other Opposition parties then met with Martin and cobbled together a deal that kept the Liberal government in office for a few more months.

In the spring of 2005, facing imminent defeat on his minority government's first budget, Prime Minister Martin reconsidered his dismissal of Layton's offer to co-operate on terms.

In a series of exchanges, teams representing the Liberal and NDP leaders (the NDP team was led by Layton's then-chief-of-staff Bob Gallagher, who had been in his position for only a few days when these discussions began) agreed on a set of measures in return for support in the house for one budget. Under the terms of the resulting "NDP budget," wasteful and unnecessary proposed spending on broad-brush corporate tax cuts was redirected into productive investment in public transit, housing, and other useful measures. Then, through a timely defection by Belinda Stronach, who was appointed to cabinet, and a key vote by independent MP Chuck Cadman acting on principle, the Martin government survived.

A good budget was passed as a result. Layton and his caucus were pleased. They thought they were finally starting to get some results in the minority Parliament, exactly as Layton had hoped. The NDP team in Parliament was therefore willing to do more business with the Martin government. But Prime Minister Martin wasn't interested.

Instead, as a senior official in Mr. Martin's Privy Council Office explained to me over lunch in the early fall of 2005, the Martin Liberals decided on a political offensive. They concluded that there was "no danger on the right" (a ludicrous conclusion, as it turned out), but that there was one on their left—us.

That being so, the Martin team's political priority was to eradicate the NDP in a late-2005 or early-2006 election campaign. To that end, in the summer of 2005, a number of Martin's politicos travelled to London to study the language and political framing used by the British Labour Party. The Liberals worked hard to court high-profile New Democrats who might be persuaded to switch parties and run as right-wing Martinite Liberals in the next federal election. And, in the fall of 2005, the Martin government began issuing a series of press releases designed to reposition itself on top of Jack Layton's NDP.

The Liberals were suddenly committed to early action on child care, cities, First Nations, the environment, safe communities, and many other issues they thought would persuade NDP voters to switch to them. Little was actually done about any of these pressing national issues, but the Martin government communications team certainly astonished many non-governmental organizations and city mayors, whose previously ignored memos and briefs were suddenly spinning out of the PMO in the form of mock–British Labour Party government press releases.

Concurrently, the federal Liberal Party was being eaten alive by an inquiry into a publicly funded political slush fund used to sponsor festivals and other events in the province of Quebec. Liberal advertising agencies and political operatives were unable to keep their fingers out of these funds—reminding me of Mr. Melenchuk's staff and their top-of-mind issue during the early days of the 1999 Saskatchewan coalition discussions. Prime Minister Martin had foolishly called a judicial inquiry into this matter in the hope that he could make his predecessor take the blame for it, and so a large posse of lawyers were now "farming the file" on nationwide television.

The federal New Democratic Party was therefore coming under growing pressure internally to stop cooperating with the Liberals.

For example, in the fall of 2005 I dropped into the Queen's Park office of Howard Hampton, then leader of our party in Ontario, to do a little party business with one of the staff there. A staffer in Hampton's office greeted me by grabbing me by the shoulders and yelling into my face, "When the *fuck* are we going to stop propping up the fucking corrupt Liberals!!??"

Good morning to you, too.

Similar questions were being asked in our caucus, and throughout our party. In particular, former federal leader Ed Broadbent—then sitting as a member of our federal caucus, having returned as MP for Ottawa Centre in the 2004 election—was becoming increasingly uncomfortable with a policy of open-ended support for Mr. Martin's government in the circumstances that were facing us in the fall of 2005.

That summer, the Supreme Court of Canada had issued a ruling in the Chaoulli case (*Chaoulli v. Quebec [Attorney General]*, issued on June 9, 2005) that seemed to give provinces a green light to privatize public medicare. Weighing his options, Layton decided to make this unfortunate, feckless, and damaging court ruling his test case with Prime Minister Martin.

Layton did his homework on this issue, carefully consulting his caucus, health experts, and my old boss Premier Romanow, who had recently issued a Royal Commission report on health care and was a determined critic of this Supreme Court decision.

Layton then offered to support the Liberal government for another brief period, provided the Martin government agreed to take some appropriate steps to ensure that Canada's public health-care system was not further eroded by the Chaoulli decision. We had in mind a reinforcement of the *Canada Health Act*.

We made this offer privately and publicly.

In response, Prime Minister Martin allowed himself to be quoted in *The Globe and Mail* telling his caucus that he would not permit the NDP to make health care an issue, because "health care is a *Liberal* issue."

That probably would have surprised Tommy Douglas. Certainly it surprised us. But perhaps it made some sort of sense from Mr. Martin's perspective.

At a first ministers' meeting in September 2004, Martin had cut a ten-year, $41-billion deal with the provinces and territories, which was intended to "fix health care for a generation." These arrangements brought the federal government closer to its traditional 50-per-cent contribution to medicare.

A more effective and progressive-minded prime minister, with a better commitment to Canada's public medicare system, would have negotiated some important conditions in return for that kind of money—an unambiguous commitment to the single-payer system, progress towards primary care, a replacement for the fee-for-service system, first steps towards a national drug program and formulary, and a real enforcement mechanism to ensure compliance with these conditions. Instead, for all intents and purposes, Martin's new federal health funding was unconditional.

Nonetheless, the Martin team seemed to feel they now owned the medicare file. They felt entitled to it. They were in no mood to "share" it with the NDP. Quite the contrary. They hoped to use it to help crack the New Democrats in the coming federal election.

At a meeting with Layton, Martin told the NDP leader that his government would consider what we were saying. He then referred the issue and the federal NDP leader to Liberal Minister of Health Ujjal Dosanjh.

If Mr. Martin had been looking for a minister who would settle Layton down and to make the issue we were raising go away, he picked the wrong guy.

Mr. Dosanjh has acknowledged on the record that, in his youth, he "dabbled with Communism." By 2005, he was a former BC New Democrat premier who had presided over a devastating electoral defeat after playing a murky role in the ousting of his predecessor, Glen Clark. This commended him to Mr. Martin, who had shown similar loyalty to his own leader with similar results. Mr. Dosanjh had now become a particularly bitter, anti-NDP hit man in his new guise as a right-wing Martinite Liberal.

Mr. Martin now nominated Mr. Dosanjh to be one of the unheralded authors of the fall of the Liberal government, after thirteen years in office.

Mr. Dosanjh made himself briefly available to Layton and his team. The Liberal health minister dismissed our caucus's concerns about the Supreme Court ruling, saying in as many words that the Martin Liberals were not going to do anything about it, notwithstanding our views. That being so, the NDP caucus concluded it could and would no longer support the Martin government, which then promptly collapsed in a parliamentary confidence vote.

Mr. Martin, it emerged, had not thought through his own "scenarios." He took our support in Parliament as an entitlement, and had no relationship with either the Conservatives or the Bloc to fall back on. His team nevertheless had felt free to target us, to boast about it, and to ignore what we had to say about the issues that might earn our support.

The public threw them out of office in the 2006 election.

For many months thereafter, Mr. Martin's team complained bitterly that their defeat in the election was all our fault. We hadn't given them the support in Parliament they were entitled to. We hadn't given them the support in the campaign that they were entitled to. We hadn't told our voters to switch from our candidates to Liberal candidates in an act of self immolation that the Liberals were entitled to profit from. We hadn't disappeared to let the Martinites romp to power as they were entitled to.

As events demonstrated, Mr. Martin and his team were entitled to nothing from the NDP or any other competing political party. Our support, like any other, had to be earned and negotiated—by talking to us, by listening to us, and by finding some compromise with us that we could accept. That's what business in any normal Parliament is all about, particularly in a minority Parliament, which is "normal" in most of the democratic world.

In addition to my duties as national campaign director during the 2006 election campaign that followed the fall of Martin's government, I co-ordinated a reformulated "scenarios committee." I asked Anne McGrath, Terry Grier, Allan Blakeney, Ed Broadbent, and Joy MacPhail to join me in this quiet work.

Anne McGrath was a senior official in Layton's office in 2006. She would be elected president of the federal party a few months after the election, and would later serve as Layton's chief of staff. She had served as the senior staff member to the national president of the Canadian Union of Public Employees—excellent training for her later political work—and brought her cool intelligence and attention to detail to bear on this project. I looked to her to anchor the committee and keep its work in order and on track.

Terry Grier, thoughtful and enjoying Layton's absolute trust, provided continuity with the 2004 committee.

Allan Blakeney was our answer to the Liberal–Eastern Canadian media trope that the NDP knows nothing about governance. He was one of Canada's outstanding experts on good government, having served in Tommy Douglas's last cabinet, played a key role in the succeeding Lloyd government, and led Saskatchewan as premier for more than ten productive, effective, scandal-free years. He had written thoughtfully about governance since, and very generously agreed to assist us in this work, helping us to remain grounded in political and policy reality when thinking about getting results in the next Parliament.

Ed Broadbent was universally trusted in our caucus and in the federal party. He had wrestled directly with these issues as federal leader, and he would help ensure that whatever we ended up doing would be widely supported in our party—never a certainty otherwise, as the growing internal Opposition to our parliamentary work with Prime Minister Martin demonstrated.

Joy MacPhail was an incisive and brilliant provincial political leader. She understood the realities of getting results in a legislature, and was hard-headed and brutally realistic about what could fly and not fly politically and in substance.

We had the base of Grier's work on the form of accords and coalitions, so our focus in 2006 was on policy. I considered this important, given the mistakes I believed the Saskatchewan Liberals had made when they entered into coalition with us in Saskatchewan in 1999.

Jean Monnet, an early architect of the European Union, used to say: "There are two categories of people: those who want to be someone, and those who want to do something." In my view, the Saskatchewan Liberals focused too enthusiastically on being "somebodies." They very badly wanted to be cabinet ministers. But they didn't put enough thought into what they wanted to do once they had earned their cabinet seats through a coalition negotiation. As a result, they hadn't thought through what accomplishments they hoped to point to when the coalition had run its course and the time had come to seek a renewed mandate from voters. The Saskatchewan Liberal Party imploded during their years in coalition in large part, in my view, because they couldn't explain even to themselves why they were in office.

Our 2006 scenarios committee had the job of weighing the same risks the Saskatchewan Liberals had chosen to take in 1999. It seemed to me we needed to learn from them, and spend some careful time thinking about what we would accomplish if we were given the same opportunity.

We were building on our experience with the 2005 NDP budget. Layton scored a solid set of accomplishments in that parliamentary agreement with Prime Minister Martin, providing us with a helpful record to point to during the 2006 election campaign. We hoped to replicate that experience somehow in the next Parliament.

So we worked away, carefully comparing our election platform (or, at least, the more realistic elements our committee members felt might be possible to work with) to the priorities and policies of Stephen Harper's Conservatives and Paul Martin's Liberals.

We were able to identify a few points in common with the Conservative Party platform. These were notably on crime and justice issues that our leader and caucus felt strongly about, and the anti-corruption, good government, and democratic reform priorities to which Mr. Harper had committed his party.

We speculated that the Harper Conservatives might be willing to discuss some form of electoral reform, a topic close to Broadbent's heart, in return for support in Parliament on justice and good-government issues, provided we could also agree on a relatively benign, neutral federal budget that did not require the NDP to vote for measures our party, movement, and voting base could not accept.

There was, nominally, more overlap with the Liberals.

They had carried many of their fall 2005 press releases into their election platform, and were therefore making commitments about health care, cities, infrastructure, Aboriginal people, and the environment (many of which had also figured in the Liberal Party's unimplemented 1993, 1997, 2000, and 2004 platforms) that we thought were bridgeable with many of our own proposals.

Our experience with Mr. Martin and his team in the final weeks of their government made us extremely skeptical that they could or would work amicably with us or anyone else on any kind of common agenda. But we gamely laboured on scenarios as directed by our federal leader, drawing up a memorandum that set out our areas of potential common ground with the Liberals and sketching what a parliamentary agreement with them might look like.

In the event, the results of the 2006 election handed Layton another relatively weak poker hand in a new minority Parliament. The Harper Conservatives took office with 124 seats. The Martin Liberals were sent into official Opposition with 102 seats. The Bloc were in a balance-of-power position with 51 seats. And we had those 29 seats—again just shy of the balance of power.

Layton discussed a few ideas with newly installed Prime Minister Harper, and the NDP supported elements of the new government's crime and governance reform. But there was no basis for a broader understanding. The Conservatives had readier partners available among the defeated ranks of the Liberals and with the Bloc Québécois.

The Bloc was particularly helpful to Mr. Harper in the first years of his government, looking forward as it did to some seriously large cash payments to the province of Quebec to fund the "fiscal imbalance," and to a significant dismantling of Canada's national government at the hands of Mr. Harper's small-government party.

Mr. Martin was succeeded in December 2006 by Stéphane Dion, and the new Liberal leader enjoyed a serviceable honeymoon. But the Liberal Party was unable to respond to a barrage of well-funded, targeted negative advertising unloaded on Dion's head by the Harper Conservatives. A charge unanswered being a charge accepted, the Harper Conservatives succeeded over the course of 2007 in defining Mr. Dion in the eyes of the public. Bizarrely, they were able to frame Dion as "weak," "indecisive," "not a leader"—areas where Dion was actually fairly strong, as his early ministerial record proved. Dion was unable to fight this campaign effectively because his party was broke and could not air counterattacks, he struggled in English (although he spoke beautifully in French), and he didn't really have a compelling message.

Dion attempted to solve the latter problem by turning to what was then the top-of-mind issue facing the country—the environment, a file he felt he knew well, having served as Martin's environment minister. Dion had staked out a sensible position on environmental issues during his leadership campaign, but, foolishly, he abandoned his own views on the topic and adopted the platform advanced during the 2006 Liberal leadership campaign by Michael Ignatieff. Thus, Dion dropped his mainstream cap-and-trade climate-change proposal and instead embraced Ignatieff's plan to radically reform the tax system in Canada, cutting income and consumption taxes and transferring the federal tax burden onto carbon emissions through a carbon tax.

Many social democrats oppose tax-shift, carbon-tax proposals in the form proposed by Ignatieff and then by Dion and the Liberal team. A basic concern is that they might work—that a radical transfer of national taxes away from income and consumption and onto carbon emissions would reduce those emissions—and thus reduce federal revenues. This would undermine the federal government's finances and thus would undermine key public services like health care and education. Ignatieff-style tax-shift, carbon-tax proponents answer that the federal government could just keep hiking its carbon tax rate. Many social democrats would answer that taxing what one hopes will be a continually dwindling supply of carbon is a thin reed on which to build public services—not dissimilar to the Alberta government's unhealthy dependence on oil and gas royalties.

Thus many of our sort prefer to keep a solid, balanced, and permanent tax system built on income and consumption taxes. This is why New Democrats advocate a cap-and-trade system, which leaves the core of the tax system alone. Carbon is given a real price, revenues are used to reward companies who reduce emissions, and over time both emissions and the revenues derived from them phase out. Ideally this will leave the rest of our civilization, including the foundations of our public services, intact. A similar approach was used to address acid rain in the 1980s.

It is for these reasons that the New Democrats rejected the Liberal tax-shift, carbon-tax plan on its merits.

The Conservatives rejected it as well, but for simpler populist reasons. The Liberals were proposing a big new tax. Seizing their opportunity, during the summer months of 2008, while Dion was stumping the country hyping his new tax, the Conservatives did their research. They filmed and aired millions of dollars worth of soft-soap ads, and then sacked the Liberals by breaking their own fixed election bill and calling an early election in September 2008.

This was excellent play by Mr. Harper and his team. The election call caught the Liberals flat-footed, without a viable campaign message and without an airplane.

Mr. Harper's election call didn't catch the NDP by surprise, however, because we understood something the Liberals did not: that the government was in control of election timing, not the Liberal Party. For months the Liberals had been giving interviews trying to defend their policy of propping up Mr. Harper in the house through abstentions by saying that "we the Liberals will decide when the next election is, and it will be called by us when we feel we're ready and the timing is convenient for us."

The NDP, on the other hand, was under no illusion that we were in control of election timing. We therefore had reactivated our election planning committee within weeks of the 2006 election, met weekly thereafter, and worked steadily at campaign preparation for almost two years. For those with the wit to read them, there were numerous signs in the summer of 2008 that an early election was on the way. We therefore had our platform ready, our ads thought through, our transport and tour pre-planned and booked, our campaign organization identified and in place, and our slate of candidates close to being completed (alas, including a few names that would better have been left off).

The campaign went well. We emerged with 37 seats, our second-largest result in our party's history. The Tories won 143 seats; the Liberals 76; the Bloc 48. We finally had a clean balance-of-power position in Parliament.

As directed by Layton, I had re-activated our scenarios committee during the course of that 2008 campaign. Terry Grier wasn't available to us, being in Europe. Joy MacPhail was busy with her career. The rest of the committee (McGrath, Blakeney, Broadbent, and I, joined by deputy campaign director Sue Milling) returned to basically the same issues.

We reviewed party election proposals and reached roughly similar conclusions as we did in the 2006 exercise. We could see some areas of common ground with the Conservatives (consumer protection, crime). We could also see somewhat more common ground with the Liberals. On the other hand, we were now going to have to deal with a fundamental policy disagreement with the Liberals, passionately committed as they were to Mr. Ignatieff's tax-shift, carbon-tax plan.

For his part, Jack Layton seemed pretty clear where he wanted this work to go. He wanted us to figure out a way to remove the Conservatives from office and to replace them with a coalition government—turning the tables on Mr. Harper by using Harper's own proposed parliamentary manoeuvres to replace him. Layton was so clear about this that he said so publicly during the campaign.

As the *Toronto Star* put it (September 22, 2008):

> *Asked on CTV's Canada AM if he would "entertain even the notion of entering into a coalition with the Liberals in order to get the Conservatives out of power," the New Democrat stressed he's never allowed partisanship to trump the greater public good.*
>
> *"Well, you know what, I've worked with any other party. I think people have seen that if they look back to my days on a municipal council," said Layton, a former Toronto councillor and one-time president of the Federation of Canadian Municipalities. "You roll up your sleeves and you try to solve a problem," he said. "I think right now the problem we have is Stephen Harper and his Conservatives. They're taking the country down the wrong path. They're much too close to a (U.S. President) George Bush style foreign policy when it comes to the war in my view."*

I mused about this statement in a diary in which I was doodling to try to keep myself sane during the campaign (September 22, 2008): "Big issue now is what will this big bomb we just dropped—talk of coalition—do to us? Could be good, especially in Ontario. Runs the pro-Harper stuff off us, alludes to arrangement the electorate really wants. Bad news will be in BC, Man., and PQ. Vote NDP = get Libs."

That turned out to be a good bet. The Conservatives pounced on Layton's trial balloon as evidence that a vote for the NDP was a vote for a return to Liberal government. Mr. Dion for his part quickly vowed that he would never, ever, consider governing in coalition with New Democrats. His strategists well understood that Layton's proposal would be popular with Liberal voters (as it remains at this writing), and they didn't want Layton to be more appealing than he already was to their dwindling base of support.

On October 4, 2008, our scenarios committee sat down to talk through our options. With Layton's coalition commitment motivating us to take these issues very seriously indeed, I outlined what I thought those options were. Given our leader's clear preference for focusing on turning the Conservatives out of office, I suggested that the best possible outcome would be an election result that gave the Liberals and the NDP in combination a majority of the house. If that were to happen, it was my view that we should propose a formal coalition to the Liberal Party, with a joint cabinet. In a way we were setting up such an offer with our election campaign, which was designed to focus exclusively on taking on the Conservatives (something we had to deviate from now and then during the campaign to parry attacks on our party and leader from the Liberals).

Allan Blakeney basically agreed that this was our best option. He supported a joint Liberal–NDP ministry in the event our caucuses added up to a majority. But he considered this majority to be highly unlikely, since in his view (quite accurately as it turned out) the Tories were headed towards about 140 seats in this election. That meant that a potential coalition government would also need support from the Bloc Québécois. Blakeney considered a direct deal with the Bloc to be political poison and preferred that the Liberals, who would benefit by leading the government, pay the price of obtaining that support. Blakeney added two key elements.

First, he noted that Dion would be likely to resign if he did poorly in the election, so timing would be key. We needed to put this opportunity to him as quickly as possible, so he could consider it before he resigned. Further, Blakeney argued, the offer should be in the form of a letter that we would make public, so that our proposals would not be mischaracterized when they became public—as they inevitably would be—and so that the Liberals would take responsibility for the continued existence of the Harper government should they refuse our proposal.

Ed Broadbent strongly supported a joint Liberal–NDP cabinet, provided the NDP entered the arrangement with some real bargaining muscle, such as a balance-of-power position. "Whenever we have the balance of power in a cabinet, we should seize it," he said. That would put the NDP in the best position to influence and drive government policy, and to ensure that New Democrats actually got some political credit for our policies and proposals. "Having ministers in positions to be seen and to get credit for what we actually do is better than influencing things from outside." Always provided that the NDP had real bargaining power, he argued that the Canadian public was looking for stability and therefore a stable coalition government would serve them well.

Anne McGrath and Sue Milling both supported the option of a "stable accord" between us and the Liberals, followed by a Liberal–Bloc accord in some form if necessary. Milling noted that our party needed a period of calm to rebuild its own electoral war chest and to be able to focus on upcoming provincial elections in British Columbia and Nova Scotia.

With this agreed, we got to work drafting a strategy note for the federal leader's eyes, and draft correspondence that could be given to both Dion and Duceppe on election night or shortly thereafter.

As election night loomed and the shape of the coming Liberal debacle became clear in our tracking and in public-domain polling, I grew more pessimistic that we would be handed the cards we needed to replace the Conservative government. But we kept working away at the file.

Election day was October 14, 2008.

Sue Milling and I met with Jack Layton in his hotel room in Toronto that afternoon. We reviewed with him our most recent tracking and a seat projection prepared by our polling firm, Viewpoints Research, which accurately predicted our final results. We were going to win between 35 and 40 seats, with a big breakthrough in Northern Ontario and new beachheads in Alberta and Newfoundland.

We then carefully reviewed the scenarios committee's recommendations. Layton listened to the options we set out, and reviewed the draft letter to be given to Dion, if circumstances warranted, proposing a common effort to remove Harper and to replace his government. Layton revised the correspondence, it was finalized, signed, and tucked away in an envelope.

Most of the senior players in our campaign joined Layton, his partner, Olivia Chow, and many members of Layton's family for an election-night watch in a holding room at The Guvernment bar and party house on the lakeshore in downtown Toronto. Not a bad name for an election-night headquarters.

I was hopeful that we might get some lucky bounces, but I was also trying to fight off a creeping undercurrent of dread. Our tracking clearly showed that we had come out of the weekend with no momentum and, in fact, were slowly bleeding votes to all our opponents. In the event, we got just about exactly what we expected—18 per cent of the vote and 37 seats.

The shocker of the evening was the Liberal numbers. With 26 per cent of the vote and 77 seats, the Liberals had been handed their worst election result (in share of votes) since Confederation. With only 114 seats between the Liberals and the NDP, compared to 143 for the Conservatives, the possibility of a majority two-party coalition government was dead. It was also hard to imagine that Stéphane Dion was going to be in the mood that night to contemplate trying to form a government on the basis of some sort of accord with us and then with the Bloc.

Nonetheless, Layton gave it a try. He called Dion when the results were clear to congratulate him on his campaign, to commiserate a little, and to see if Dion was in any mood to discuss what options might lie before Parliament. Dion was clearly appalled by the results, and told Layton that now was not the time to explore those options. Perhaps the topic could be discussed later. Minutes later, he appeared on television to accept responsibility for his party's performance. He would resign as Liberal leader two days later, but would also elect to remain as interim leader until he could be replaced at a leadership convention.

After his call to Dion, Layton compared notes with his senior advisors. We all agreed that there was no obvious window to pursue "scenarios," given these results and the way Dion was reacting to them. So we tucked our letter to Mr. Dion away. Layton made the best he could of the results in an election-night statement to a somewhat glum crowd of Toronto NDP partisans—and it was time for me to hang up my national campaign director hat and go back home.

I had signed up for a five-week stint in our 2004 campaign war room. Instead, I had spent four years of major after-hours volunteer time helping to steer our election team and many months living in hotel rooms in Ottawa during three national campaigns. I was game to continue to be tapped for project work (all of this being so darn much fun), but it was time for the party to find a new national campaign director. Layton's parliamentary and party staff had matured into a tight and highly competent team. I knew they could do this work by themselves. Brad Lavigne, director of policy and communications in the leader's office, was appointed to succeed me as national campaign director.

My bet was that we were now in for a relatively stable "Pearson minority" under Mr. Harper and that federal politics was likely to be fairly quiet for a while.

But that isn't what happened.

Jack Layton has an extraordinary ability to recover from election campaigns, to find his bearings, and to begin quickly to look for ways to work with whatever political hand he is dealt.

It seems clear that Mr. Layton held to his view, spelled out during the 2008 campaign, that the majority that had just been elected to serve in the new Parliament had a duty to combine, to remove Mr. Harper from office, and to install a better, progressive government in tune with the views of the majority of the Canadian people and with the views of the majority of MPs sitting in the House of Commons.

Layton did not indulge in the high-decibel personal demonization of Mr. Harper heard from Liberals during campaigns (an example, for the neo-cons among the red team, of the narcissism of small differences). He knew Mr. Harper, respected him as a skilful opponent, and understood that over-the-top hysterics ultimately worked to Mr. Harper's advantage.

But he strongly believed that Mr. Harper and his ministry were fundamentally wrong about the fiscal, economic, social, and foreign-policy issues facing the country. And he strongly believed that Canada would be better served by a new, better coalition government that would reverse Mr. Harper's high-deficit, anti-worker, recessionary, regressive, pro-war policies, and pursue better priorities.

Like Ed Broadbent, Layton believed that, by taking cabinet seats in such a government, New Democrats would ensure that a progressive agenda would not only be promised, but would be implemented as well—a helpful change from the Liberal-only cabinets of the recent past.

Layton also believed that there were better prospects for success than many of us on his team could see. He was reasonably sure, for example, that Gilles Duceppe and the Bloc Québécois were now ready to drop their support of the Conservative government and to help replace Mr. Harper.

The Quebec labour movement, Layton knew, was increasingly unhappy with the Harper regime and with the Bloc Québécois's role in keeping it in office. The Bloc listened closely to Quebec unions and to their federations, notably the Quebec Federation of Labour (FTQ).

Further, the 2008 election had pitted Harper's Conservatives against Duceppe's Bloc head-to-head in Quebec, making it less likely the Bloc would support the Conservatives in the resulting Parliament and reducing their political interest in doing so. Some back-channelling after the 2008 election confirmed this: the Bloc was willing to consider working with us to replace the Harper Conservatives.

Layton therefore began to look for ways to open a dialogue with the Liberals.

As part of that effort, he asked me as his 2008 campaign chair to see if I could have a few words with Senator David Smith, the 2008 Liberal campaign chair, and an opportunity to do so presented itself on October 21, 2008, during a panel organized by the Public Affairs Association of Canada at the Albany Club in downtown Toronto.

I sent Layton a BlackBerry report about how that went (October 21, 2008):

> As discussed I appeared on a panel today with some interesting company—Senator Hugh Segal and Senator David Smith. The panel was a "post mortem" on the election. Pretty tame stuff and no real news out of it. Senator Smith and I then had an offline chat. After a pleasant exchange of anecdotes and stories (many about Lester Pearson in his case) we got down to business:
>
> I told him I was a little sorry that Mr. Dion was staying on as Liberal leader since that made it difficult for people in Parliament who might have been thinking of kicking the Tories out. He clearly knew exactly what I was talking about. He replied that whether or not Dion remained during the interregnum, the Liberals will be fully engaged in the next leadership race and could not contemplate anything ambitious in the house.
>
> I probed him a little, suggesting the Liberals might find themselves in an uncomfortable position when the session resumes. He basically shrugged and said (a) the public doesn't expect anyone to defeat a government over a Throne Speech and (b) any negatives they might get for letting Harper govern will be reset once they have a new leader.
>
> He seemed to enjoy our chat. We agreed there needed to be a better channel between our parties. There was a faint suggestion that something might be possible after the convention. We agreed to stay in touch. I think this probably is a pretty good read on what the Libs are thinking now. So it still seems correct to focus on our "ask" for this coming session and to await events.

Layton replied: "Your report makes sense when we consider their perspective and the project that lies ahead of them."

And that was that . . . until Prime Minister Harper intervened.

Part Two
The Coalition Negotiations

Wednesday,
November 26, 2008

Just before 6:00 p.m., my BlackBerry buzzed. It was an e-mail from Jack Layton.

"CTV is reporting that the per-voter public financing scheme is to be cancelled in tomorrow's update," he wrote. "I believe that the Liberals could be tempted by our earlier proposition, faced with such a catastrophic proposal. Self-preservation could provoke out-of-the-box thinking. I would like to discuss having you re-open your line of communication with your contact."

This was a more than interesting e-mail.

In the fall of 2008, *CTV News* tended to be relatively accurate in their news breaks about what the Harper government was planning to do. The network had played an important role in eviscerating Stéphane Dion's fall 2008 campaign. The CTV team seemed to have excellent sources in the Prime Minister's Office—and CTV political correspondent Mike Duffy was a few weeks away from being appointed to the Senate as a Conservative.

So when CTV reported that the Conservatives were planning to bankrupt the Opposition parties, we needed to take the news seriously.

The federal New Democratic Party had emerged from the fall 2008 election with a net debt of over $4 million. Our repayment plan for that debt was built on public financing introduced by Jean Chrétien to try to break the power of corporate money in his own Liberal Party—and of union funding in ours. This reform, designed to get "big money" out of politics, was proposed by the Canadian Democracy and Corporate Accountability Commission co-chaired by Ed Broadbent in January 2002.

Here's how that system works. The idea is that political parties should win the resources they need from the contributions and votes of citizens, not from corporations, single-interest groups, or trade unions. We know what a political system corrupted by money from special interests looks like. It looks like the Philippines under Marcos. Or like our friendly neighbour south of the border.

To avoid a similar fate, in 2003 Parliament adopted a law banning big-money political contributions from corporations and unions, and it replaced those funds in part with funding derived from how many votes political parties earn—the more votes, the more funding (distributed at the rate of about $1.75 per vote, annually). This system disempowers bagmen, and focuses Canadian political parties where they should be focused: on earning the support of Canadian voters.

Chrétien's reform had worked. His party was no longer funded by Bay Street—and we could no longer rely on funding from the labour movement. So we financed our campaigns through a healthy and growing base of small-scale donations, through loans, and through an eighteen- to twenty-four-month post-campaign repayment plan.

This being so, the case—an abrupt and retroactive cancellation of public funding, as proposed by Mr. Harper—might make it challenging for us to confront the Conservatives in the next election. The Liberals, Layton figured, were in the same boat.

Attacking the finances of the Opposition and returning politics to big money was what made the news about the November 2008 Conservative economic statement. But there was much else there to object to. The Tories proposed to strip federal public servants of their right to strike. They proposed to abolish pay equity for women working in the federal public service. But perhaps the worst element of the Tory economic statement was its silences. The world economy in the fall of 2008 was being battered by a global financial crisis. A deep recession followed. Canada's manufacturing and resource industries were cracking.

The Harper Conservatives had a plan to address these issues. They proposed to do nothing.

I took a bit of time before replying to our federal leader's e-mail. I had to get my mind around the idea we were going to try to reactivate our coalition proposal.

On the one hand, the federal Liberals were in worse financial shape than we were, and would have to look at their options again in light of Harper's attempt to bankrupt them. Indeed all three Opposition parties now had an immediate, compelling, and concurrent reason to co-operate to rid the country of Mr. Harper. All the Opposition parties were also likely to agree that the Harper government had failed to address the economic crisis, and this created the basis for an understanding about the core priorities of a new and better government.

On the other hand, I just didn't believe we had an interested partner. I had never heard any Liberal in any forum ever say that they supported "our earlier proposition." I didn't believe they were interested or would ever be interested.

However, when your federal leader asks you to do something, it's generally fit and proper to do it. So, in mid-evening, I gave Senator Smith a call and left a message on his voice mail, which was not returned.

"Can't raise my friend. You might be able to get this talk going faster tomorrow via house leader channel, or c-o-s [chief of staff]," I wrote at 11:46 p.m. "I'll try him again later this morning just for fun, though."

I was skeptical that Senator Smith would be a useful channel through which to talk to the Liberals—and indeed he was not. It seemed to me that talking to Ralph Goodale (Stéphane Dion's house leader) or to Johanne Sénécal (his chief of staff) would attract the inevitable Liberal brush-off more quickly.

Thursday,
November 27, 2008

JACK LAYTON WASTED NO TIME PURSUING THIS ISSUE.

"What is the state of the 'letter' that we had been considering sending to the political leaders?" Layton asked me at 7:24 a.m. via his BlackBerry. "Was there a list of legislative initiatives that would form the basis of a relationship?"

"Clearly it [our draft letter] needs a substantial revision," I replied at 7:31 a.m. "Its focus was our 08 platform with biggest move being child benefit. What we need here is an economic focus. Toughest deal point remains the corporate tax cuts, which both Dion and Rae said they still support. Our draft proposes to indefinitely postpone these."

That morning's newspapers were full of the story that Mr. Harper was going to move to bankrupt the Opposition. But I still didn't believe this issue would move the Liberals from their track towards their leadership convention and towards our proposal.

Here's why:

At its core, I thought, the federal Liberal Party is the voice of the Eastern English–Canadian family compact, the snug and affluent little world that gets its party pictures printed in the pages of *Toronto Life* and the *Toronto Star*, lives in Rosedale, Etobicoke, and Oakville, and works in office buildings within ten blocks of the corner of Bay and King in Toronto. And their more widely-scattered allies in the business leadership of Toronto's ethnic communities and of Montreal, and dwindling islands of upper-middle-class activists in cities across the rest of the country.

Theirs is one of the industrialized world's increasingly rare post–World War II brokerage parties, such as the former Christian Democrats in Italy, the Liberal Democrats in Japan, and the PRI in Mexico. Like them (as Stephen Harper put it in an interesting article, "Our Benign Dictatorship," co-authored with Tom Flanagan and published in the winter 1996/1997 edition of *Next City*), the Liberal Party brings together individuals interested in exercising power and dispensing patronage.

If Mr. Harper was now going to smash Mr. Chrétien's rules and reintroduce big money to Canadian politics, these people were not lacking in fundraising ability. The Liberal Party establishment had strongly opposed Mr. Chrétien's reforms when he introduced them (Liberal Party President Stephen LeDrew called them "dumb as a bag of hammers"). I thought the federal Liberals might privately welcome the opportunity to return to banks and oil companies for their funding, and would therefore arrange to have Mr. Harper's economic statement pass.

Jack Layton saw things differently.

After reading the paragraphs above in an earlier draft of these notes, Layton argued that they fail to capture the full reality of the federal Liberal Party. That party, he believes, is fundamentally made up of two wings. One—usually small and weak—believes in "positive liberty," in an active role for government to make people's lives better, without otherwise affecting the political and economic status quo. The other wing—the much stronger and more influential one—believes in "negative liberty," in defending people's legal and human rights, perhaps in extending their equality of opportunity, but not in active steps to promote broader equality itself. Thus, the party consists of a feeble and usually marginalized group of "left Liberals" (people strongly influenced by their churches, for example), and a strong group of "business Liberals" who call the shots.

In Layton's view, when the Liberal Party is out of power, the dominant wing "will accept a more progressive agenda if it is the only route to power, and they have no other choice. They will let that happen to get to power."

Layton was about to offer them that opportunity. He believed there was a finite but real chance to get some of the NDP's agenda advanced through some form of coalition with the Liberals. For the New Democrats, there were "no other tools on the table," given the nature of the Harper government and the correlation of forces in Parliament as they existed after the 2008 election.

And, as we were about to learn, Liberal leadership politics were going to help open a brief window of opportunity for us to move forward.

"If the Senator is in Ottawa, I or others could meet him if needed," Layton wrote back at 7:36 a.m. that morning. Layton's run for mayor of Toronto earlier in his career had been blocked in part by some manoeuvring by Senator Smith ("sharp practice" is how Allan Blakeney might have called what Layton believes Smith did to him in that campaign). Layton didn't want to let go of Smith as a channel for poetic as well as practical reasons, I think.

"Also, what do you think of a public call for a coalition if the economic update does not include dramatic action on an economic stimulus? The media will say we're doing it because of the cut to party financial, of course. But if we stay the course, we can weather that storm because of the economic news, and how the coalition handles it will dominate the news over time."

This was good political analysis by our leader, and one I found persuasive then and now. The prime minister had called an election that fall in direct violation of his own fixed-elections law. Nobody cared on election day. Canada was now facing a dangerous economic crisis. If the Conservatives focused on playing political games instead of addressing that crisis, we might be able to dump and replace them, and then drown out the inevitable backlash from the Conservative Party's anger machine by controlling the government agenda and—we hoped—doing a better job.

"Key in all of this is who is the PM?" I replied (7:44 a.m.). I was warming up. "That requires a prior conversation with the Libs. If they agree it can be Goodale or McCallum, then this has some legs. If they insist it must be Dion, then you are probably holding a busted flush given Bloc won't play."

I was pointing out here that we did not have the numbers between the Liberals and NDP to unseat Harper, and that the Bloc seemed unlikely to me to be interested in installing the author of the *Clarity Act* as prime minister in place of the decentralizing Harper Conservatives.

Layton knew better, having been given a clear idea of where the Bloc was coming from. "I don't believe the Bloc will be in as strong a position as they were a few weeks ago in opposing Dion as PM," he wrote (8:14 a.m.) "They will be very concerned about losing the public funding and they will be seized with the importance of strong action on EI and stimulus. Standing in the way of a new government because of their attitude towards Dion could be very damaging to them. I will meet with Dion and propose that he consider the scenario, based upon a lack of economic stimulus and the anti-democratic nature of the proposal to cancel, essentially retroactively, the funding of the democratic process— bringing in the era of big-money politics again."

I was pleased Layton was going to deal directly with Dion, going straight to the Liberal leader without any further dancing, so that we could get our "no thanks" and get back to work.

My phone and e-mail buzzed all day with speculation and rumour. I collected it, skeptically.

The Liberal caucus met that afternoon, and I kept an eye on CBC

Newsworld to see what the Liberals might say. In due course, Stéphane Dion stepped in front of the cameras to announce that his caucus would end their support for Stephen Harper in the House of Commons, and would vote against the Conservative government's economic statement.

"He said the Liberals are voting against. It would seem this might be real!" I wrote to Layton and McGrath (4:52 p.m.). "Indeed," Layton replied (4:56 p.m.). "I intend to meet him tonight to start the process. He's saying no because he knows our option can work and that Duceppe will support it. Good job we were prepared."

McGrath also commented (4:55 p.m.): "Gadzooks!"

Gadzooks indeed.

Some of the day's random rumour-mongering now seemed worth reporting. So I sent a further little report, with a process kicker.

"Back channels: Rae and his people don't want bitter Liberal memories of the Peterson accord and its consequences to stick to him, so he's keeping his head down so far internally," I wrote to Layton and McGrath (5:02 p.m.). "Iggy folks also reserving, awaiting developments. If this gets real I think you'll want to assemble whatever you have in mind as your working group in Ottawa tomorrow."

What Bob Rae and Michael Ignatieff thought about all of this was, of course, critically important. Stéphane Dion had resigned as Liberal leader. Rae and Ignatieff were the leading candidates to succeed him. If they supported the coalition proposal, it had some sort of a chance. If not, it didn't.

I then suggested that Mr. Layton think about his working group. I knew what I wanted. I wanted the members of our "scenarios committee" to be the core of our bargaining team, since we had spent many hours thinking about this idea. Alternatively, I wanted to be cleanly severed from the process, so that I could stop thinking about it.

"Start booking the flights," Layton replied at 5:08 p.m.

But it couldn't work quite that easily.

Over the years, the NDP has experimented with a number of models in its federal leader's office. There has been a chief of staff or a principal secretary for decades. That person's role and responsibilities has morphed in many ways as succeeding leaders went through their arcs and different people came and went in the job.

I liked what I had seen at work in Premier Romanow's office under the two chiefs of staff I had reported to (Garry Aldridge and then Judy Samuelson, both tough, smart, nimble, and inspiring staff leaders in their own ways). In my view, New Democrat leaders' offices do their best work when co-ordinated by a strong chief of staff. This being my view, I wasn't hopping on any planes unless I was asked to do so by Layton's chief of staff. I would not work at cross-purposes with her. If she didn't want me around (which would have been perfectly reasonable in the interests of clarity and unity of purpose on her team), then I wasn't going.

"Nothing will happen here without a clear signal from you—let me know," I wrote to Anne McGrath (5:23 p.m.).

"[Director of operations] Jess is calling you to make arrangements," she replied (5:34 p.m.).

Righto. I was hired, presumably for some role in the negotiating working group, details to follow. I figured this was going to be fun. So, late that afternoon, I turned a little more seriously to it.

Over the past three federal elections, I had got to know some of the strategists on Stephen Harper's team. Some of this was Opposition-party camaraderie, some of it was personalities. Among the Conservative staffers were relaxed, friendly Western and Atlantic Canadians who were easy to talk to and joke with, somewhat in contrast to the intense, occasionally bitter and hostile Torontonian-flavoured Liberal staffers. It takes "new Torontonians" like me a little while to get used to the loathing many of that city's Liberals and New Democrats seem to reserve for each other, although there is a familiar ring to it. Hunting Liberals is a tradition in Saskatchewan (similar to duck season).

That afternoon I decided to throw a few pebbles at the blue team to see how serious they were about their widely reported program, and to give them fair notice that something big was coming.

I picked a friend I had good reason to believe was close to the prime minister's thinking, and sent him a brief note (5:43 p.m.): "My folks just pushed the red button. I'm on a 7:00 a.m. flight to Ottawa."

He bit (5:56 p.m.): "Do some polling first . . . what do your voters (not activists or insiders) think about government giving $26 million to political parties during a recession?"

I replied (5:57 p.m.): "There isn't going to be an election."

He knew what that meant (5:59 p.m.): "You're gonna run the government with separatists?"

In hindsight, I should have thought more carefully about the implications of that question. From the first moment that those on Mr. Harper's team turned their minds to the prospect of a combined Opposition coalition, they knew that its key vulnerability was the role of the Bloc Québécois. They zeroed in on this in their nimble campaign against the coalition the following week, and handily won the battle for public opinion in English Canada at the price of their immediate hopes in Quebec.

My assumption was that Harper was committed to finding his majority in Quebec, and saw his constituency there in the nationalist-bleu vote currently parked with the Bloc. Further, I knew that Harper himself had proposed a coalition arrangement to both the NDP and the Bloc during Paul Martin's minority—a proposal on which Jack Layton pulled the plug.

I didn't fully appreciate that the prime minister was perfectly capable of tossing away his near-term prospects in Quebec if that was expedient. And that he and his team were capable of (to call things what they are) bald-faced lying, denying his own discussions with the Bloc and making the Quebec separatist party the flash point in the debate. Had I understood this, I would have pushed very hard indeed to keep the Bloc much farther away from any of the coalition negotiations and away from the coalition public announcement, looking instead for a separate, unilateral statement of support Mr. Duceppe could have made a day or two after the coalition was announced.

This may have been our fundamental strategic mistake. And there it was in my Tory friend's e-mail on the first day.

Tabarnacle!

Irrelevantly, I replied (6:08 p.m.): "All three Opposition leaders have said in the past two hours that they will vote against this package. This is starting to remind me of the fall of Clark's government in Christmas 1980 [actually 1979]. At a certain point the train leaves the station."

Back at me (6:13 p.m.): "I hope you don't think I'm being glib but I hope you aren't misjudging what average folks think about public subsidy of political parties. This may end up being more like Elizabeth May in the debates than Joe Clark. My plane is taking off . . . "

This was a politely drafted, but pointed jibe, as my Conservative colleague knew well—and knew I would appreciate.

In the run-up to the fall 2008 election, Green Party leader Elizabeth May waged a relentless campaign, aimed at the dwindling ranks of Liberal-friendly media and at polling companies, to crowbar her way into the Leaders' Debate. Having never elected an MP, the Green Party had no business being in that debate, but she played her hand skilfully.

Unimpressed by this, the Conservative, Bloc, and NDP debate negotiators all opposed including Ms. May in the leadership debates, since she did not qualify to be there without one elected MP. I was the NDP negotiator and was responsible for this decision for our party. After much debate, the networks decided to see it our way.

When this became public during the campaign, our federal party voters, members, candidates, and MPs made it unambiguously clear that they did not agree with me about this matter. New Democrats are always sympathetic to pleas (even the occasional bogus plea) for inclusion and democracy, and do not take well to any suggestion that their party might be conspiring with Mr. Harper's team about anything. Jack Layton overruled me from the airplane and withdrew our party's objection to Ms.

May's inclusion in the debate, forcing the Conservatives to do the same.

Later that day, I took responsibility for this debacle at a meeting of our entire campaign staff and apologized to campaign press spokesperson Brad Lavigne and to our phone-bank staff for the hell I had made them endure during the preceding forty-eight hours.

The Conservatives said to me privately that this affair proved that our party "doesn't know how to take a punch," and that we foolishly did not understand that process stories don't last. In other words, our party had panicked for no good reason.

My friend was now suggesting we were doing so again.

Other people on Harper's team let us know through other channels that they assumed the NDP would see the net benefit to us of bankrupting the Liberal Party.

This was a miscalculation. Our leader saw a more immediate prospect, which was to use Mr. Harper's political coup/economic statement as a means to unite the Opposition, to defeat the Conservatives in the House of Commons, and to replace them with Canada's first partially NDP federal government—his basic goal as federal leader. Even if he hadn't seen it that way, concurrent Conservative proposals to eliminate pay equity for women and to suspend the right to strike in the public sector ensured our party could and would not support it.

In political work it is critical to keep lines of communication open to other parties, especially in a complex parliamentary crisis. Being attentive to this might have helped the Conservatives predict the effect of their November economic update. In a similar vein, these brief exchanges with Harper's team were far more useful than I understood at the time. What I got out of them was that the Conservatives were indeed planning to blow up public financing of political parties, and so they had indeed given us a gift: compelling motives for the Opposition parties to combine.

I was working late that night, and news kept coming in from Ottawa.

At 6:46 p.m., NDP press secretary Karl Bélanger reported: "Just bumped into Pierre-Paul, senior Bloc official. Duceppe just off the phone with Dion. He's going for it."

I reported to Layton and McGrath at 7:05 p.m.: "Senator Smith just called me. No real news—he just wanted to report his team is thinking about our proposal."

At 9:02 p.m., Anne McGrath e-mailed a report about Ed Broadbent. Jack Layton was trying to touch base with him. "No need for you [Layton] to call him. We just spoke. There is a caucus revolt brewing in the Libs to replace Dion with Iggy. . . . Said that he was told that you were opposed to either Rae or Iggy in your conversations with Dion. [Broadbent] found that hard to believe. I confirmed this was not true. You have said nothing about the leadership of their party. That's up to them. Sounds like Dion's trying to hang on now. The basis of our agreement should be an economic stimulus package. Chrétien is going out of the country on Saturday but will stay in touch with Ed."

Much of what would happen in the next four days was prefigured in this report. As was later widely reported in the media, Ed Broadbent and Jean Chrétien engaged in a number of discussions leading up to and during the coalition negotiations. They found common cause on the coalition's central elements very quickly, as McGrath reported. The incubus in the Liberal Party was also immediately visible—Michael Ignatieff's revolt against his leader.

There was a little more on this theme. Raymond Guardia, a colleague of mine at ACTRA, is, during his hobby time, a highly effective and respected senior NDP player. He ran the NDP war room in the 2006 and 2008 elections. In 2007, he took a leave to serve as campaign manager in an Outremont by-election, miraculously and very helpfully won by the NDP. He reported a conversation with Outremont NDP MP Tom Mulcair (10:19 p.m.): "Says it is for real. Libs dumping Dion. Iggy will be leader."

As it happened, Ontario Minister of Finance Dwight Duncan was holding a fundraiser at the Royal York Hotel that night. Several of my ACTRA colleagues from film and television were attending to show the flag for our industry tribe. They called me from the event to report that a number of federal Liberals were present, notably, a number of people from Michael Ignatieff's leadership campaign. Given all the news about Mr. Ignatieff, it seemed helpful to see what they might have on their minds.

So, a bit later that evening, I walked over to the Royal York Hotel and slipped into the fundraiser. At the event was my good friend and long-time film industry colleague the Honourable Doug Frith. A former Turner-era cabinet minister, he was for many years Hollywood's lead lobbyist in Canada. Thus, our work connection. He and I had kibitzed casually about an NDP–Liberal coalition a number of times. That night he introduced me to a couple of Mr. Ignatieff's key campaign aides. On the floor of the event and then at the Royal York's Library Bar, we settled down to what turned into an almost-two-hour discussion, punctuated by calls and e-mails to Jack Layton on my part and (from what I could tell) to Mr. Ignatieff on their part.

At 11:12 p.m. I reported what I was hearing from the Ignatieff team to Layton and McGrath. "They say they have 57 MPs on board. On its face they say they will win the first ballot. Do they want to risk that? I said why risk an election when you can be in office now? They heard we opposed Ignatieff as the PM. I called you on that. Told them from 'highest authority' otherwise unattributed what you said. Possibility is, I guess, that we end up having to deal with Iggy."

This was a somewhat garbled report about a conversation that went on in three acts.

In the first part of the conversation, my new acquaintances from the Ignatieff campaign asked me to explain to them why they should be supportive of a coalition with the NDP at all. In their view, they had a crushing majority of the Liberal caucus behind them, and they were confident that Michael Ignatieff would win on the first ballot at the planned May 2009 Liberal leadership campaign. They could then expect a nice bump in the polls during Ignatieff's honeymoon. They could defeat Harper in the house in the spring or fall of 2009, defeat him again in the subsequent election, and then they'd be in office nice and clean, the old, traditional way. As it later turned out, they never really deviated from this strategy.

I replied by pointing out that, as long as the Bloc Québécois was viable, they were not going to win a majority government in any conceivable scenario—a view with which they agreed. This being so, I argued, why go through a year's political work with all of its uncertainty, hoping to end up at the head of a minority government, when you could have exactly that outcome next week?

They took a little pause to make a series of phone calls to their mother ship.

In the second part of the conversation, they asked me very directly about who would be the prime minister of such a government. Specifically, was it true that Jack Layton had told Stéphane Dion that only Dion would be acceptable to us? As noted above, Ed Broadbent had also heard that one.

I called Layton to ask him what I should say in reply. He told me to inform Mr. Ignatieff's people that the NDP took no position on who the Liberal leader and prime minister should be. That was up to the Liberals to decide.

This answer seemed to please Ignatieff's people a great deal, and they took a time out to make some more calls.

In the third part of the conversation, on their return, their tone changed markedly. They were suddenly a good deal less friendly. Their message was that we would see what would happen in coming days. They provided some contact numbers, and then they left to join the rest of their team.

I had a couple of glasses of wine with my film industry friends and then called it a night.

It was a long walk through empty downtown Toronto streets, surrounded by brightly lit skyscrapers, from the Royal York to my car back at my office on the corner of Church and Bloor. The walk sobered me up.

I wondered how good this was all going to look in the morning.

Friday,
November 28, 2008

SITTING ON THE RUNWAY AT PEARSON AIRPORT WAITING TO take off for Ottawa, I was peppered by e-mails from one of the Ignatieff campaign team members I had met the previous night.

7:02 a.m.: "Question: Is it coalition or nothing? What about what you did in 2004?"

Ignatieff's strategist was wondering if we would accept being outside the government, and simply doing a one-off agreement to vote for a Liberal budget in return for some wins. We had done this with Prime Minister Paul Martin on the spring 2005 budget. But it wasn't what our party was looking for now.

I replied (7:09 a.m.): "I guess we'll talk about anything. But my sense of our folks is they would strongly prefer a coalition. And my pitch to you . . . is that our folks will be better partners inside than outside. 04 scenario implies (a) an escalating set of demands to justify continued support; (b) a dismount strategy; and (c) an election campaign with a design you might find unhelpful. A coalition is a very different road."

He replied (7:13 a.m.): "Gotcha. Last question. Can a governing strategy await the defeat of the government? That is, the Tories are obviously going to say 'Jack et al are in secret back-room talks, it's anti-democratic,' and so on. Can we avoid that by focusing on their defeat first?" I see now that there was a great deal of good sense in this question. We committed several political sins in the following few days, in addition to giving the Bloc Québécois an overly prominent role.

First, as Mr. Dion did with the Ignatieff tax-shift, carbon-tax proposal during the 2008 election campaign, we made ourselves the issue. Wise oppositions keep the focus on the government.

Second, we gave Prime Minister Harper and his skilful team time to think about the challenge we were mounting and to devise countermoves that ultimately prevailed. Perhaps we should have played a much cooler game, not revealing whether or not we would collectively defeat the government (to keep the focus on them, and their focus on trying to survive the vote). And then perhaps we could have sprung an accord on them in a way that left them no time to react.

I wrote (7:29 a.m.): "If Libs/Ignatieff can't say with confidence that they can govern with a majority of MPs committed to vote supply, then risk is GG might grant Harper an election."

How did I know that? I didn't, although giving comfort to the governor general had been talked about carefully in our scenarios committee. In my view, we needed to lock up the coalition and a new majority in the house, signed and sealed, as quickly as possible and as the first priority— as Premier Romanow had done in Saskatchewan in 1999. With this in place, I thought, it might not matter what the Conservatives did. Our new government would be reasonably sure of being given a chance to govern, and then could earn a mandate by doing a good job.

In fact, given that the election had been held only weeks before, the governor general might well have responded to the defeat of Harper's economic statement by asking the Liberal leader (whoever that might have been) to try to form a new government, whether or not he had a coalition accord in public view. If so, we could have done our coalition negotiating with the Conservatives safely defeated and unable to react as effectively as they did.

Tempting.

But by then, Mr. Dion would have been couped by Mr. Ignatieff. And Mr. Ignatieff and his team had (it turned out) no interest in striking an accord with us at any time or on any terms. So, in part for reasons I didn't see that morning, our only real shot was to go for the ring quickly and with the current Liberal leader.

I landed in Ottawa, and told the cab driver to leave me off on Wellington Street in front of the eternal flame at the foot of Parliament Hill. Armed with a staff security badge I had been issued during the fall election, I walked up the main walkway and into the Parliament buildings through the main doors under the Peace Tower. I was trying to generate some good luck. It was time for our tribe to stop entering through the side doors.

Jack Layton occupies a suite of offices in a storied sixth-floor corridor of the Centre Block on Parliament Hill. Among other party saints who had worked in those offices was Stanley Knowles, who had waged his lifelong campaign for decent pensions for Canadians in those rooms. I said hello to Jack Layton and to Anne McGrath, who were getting ready for a critical, face-to-face meeting with Stéphane Dion. Layton invited me to use his office while he met with Mr. Dion, so I spread out on his conference table and started in on the phones.

My first call was to Robin Sears.

Sears has had an interesting career. He is one of my predecessors as our party's national campaign director. He was also one of the architects of the party's revival in the 1980s and of its most successful previous run for office, under Ed Broadbent. He has worked as an official at Socialist International, giving him contacts in progressive parties all around the world. As chief of staff to Bob Rae, he was one of the architects of the rise of the Ontario NDP to office in 1990. He had worked as a provincial official in international trade, centered in Hong Kong. He had worked as a senior executive search manager, giving him contacts with the upper crust of the business establishment. And he now worked as a principal at Navigator Communications, a consulting and lobbying firm heavily weighted with Harris-era Conservative operatives—with Sears as the social-democratic balance wheel. He had quietly given me a great deal of helpful advice in the past two federal election campaigns, and he would accurately warn me of many of the potholes we were about to drive into in the coalition negotiations.

We had a heads-up that Ignatieff would be making a statement later that morning. Given the concluding tone of the discussion the previous night, my concern was that Ignatieff had decided to come out publicly against Layton's initiative before our federal leader could even discuss it with Mr. Dion. At my request, Sears got in touch with the Ignatieff campaign team and arranged for me to talk to the senior campaign official who was about to sit down at his computer to write Ignatieff's statement.

What followed was a blunt and frank conversation, covering much of the same ground I had reviewed with his campaign colleagues at the Duncan fundraiser the previous night and by e-mail that morning. The Ignatieff campaign was confident they would win the Liberal leadership in May. Why would they want to risk that through a totally novel political agreement with us? Further, my contact argued, they were "not sure it is legitimate to take over the government" without a mandate from a delegated leadership convention and then an election.

I reiterated my basic point: there was no reasonable prospect of any party getting a majority in another election, so to pass up this opportunity is to choose to work for a year in the hope of getting what is available next week. I urged that Mr. Ignatieff not kill this initiative.

My contact eventually concluded by saying he was of a mind to recommend the following: that Mr. Ignatieff would say he was not angling to be prime minister; that he would "look again" at the opportunities before the Liberal Party if the Conservatives were defeated in the House of Commons, as he would urge; and that he would be "open to a draft" in the event the Liberals decided they needed a new leader.

That's not quite what Ignatieff ended up saying, but the key point was what he didn't say. He didn't say that he rejected the idea of the Opposition combining to replace the government. That gave us a window to work on the project.

With this business dealt with as best as it could be, I spent the next hour or so alone in Layton's office reviewing our scenarios committee work, doodling in my notebook, and trying to remember everything I could about how we had pulled off the coalition in Saskatchewan.

I called Ed Broadbent and Allan Blakeney, asking (begging) them to join us in Ottawa to help lead our work on these files. Very luckily for our party, both agreed to do so. Blakeney hopped on an airplane from Saskatoon almost immediately.

Layton and McGrath returned from their meeting with Dion after about an hour and a half. The meeting had gone extremely well from Layton's perspective. Mr. Dion had quickly agreed to enter into negotiations with the NDP and the Bloc on Layton's proposal. There would be two sets of exploratory talks later that day, one between the Liberals and the NDP, the other between the Liberals and the Bloc. If it looked as if an all-Opposition agreement was possible, then detailed discussions would take place over the weekend with a view to an announcement on Monday.

Layton and Dion had then discussed the swirl of rumours on the Hill about who the NDP might be willing and not willing to work with. Specifically, Dion asked Layton about a claim that the NDP had said it would not work with Mr. Dion in a coalition. Layton told the Liberal leader that this was false; it was up to the Liberals to decide on their leadership. He reminded Dion that he had called Dion directly himself to make this proposal.

Layton also reminded Dion of what he had said about Dion at the NDP's 2006 convention in Quebec City, a few months before the Liberal leadership race.

What Layton had said at that convention was that Dion was "a man of principle and conviction, and therefore almost certain *not* to be elected leader of the Liberal Party." He had endured a measure of teasing about this statement after Dion was elected Liberal leader in December 2006. (As did I, since, as a mercifully small number of NDP insiders knew, I had suggested those words.)

That line about Dion was rooted in a conversation I had sat in on one evening at 24 Sussex Drive between Premier Roy Romanow and Prime Minister Jean Chrétien. Romanow and Chrétien had much to discuss that night, for the federal government was considering referring some key questions to the Supreme Court. These arose from the 1995 Quebec referendum and the Parti Québécois's "boil them like lobsters" stealth strategy towards breaking up the country.

Shouldn't referendum questions about partitioning Canada be clear? Shouldn't there be a substantial majority in favour before a partition proposal goes forward? Would a unilateral declaration of independence by the Quebec national assembly be legal or binding? Shouldn't proposed partitions (of Canada and of Quebec) be negotiated? Chrétien was still weighing the wisdom of putting those issues to the Supreme Court.

Romanow strongly urged that the federal government do so, and offered to intervene in the proceedings with a supportive brief (Premier Gary Filmon's government in Manitoba would do so as well). Romanow would keep that commitment after the federal government decided to proceed with the reference. Our government's legal brief, elegantly written by Saskatchewan Deputy Minister of Justice John Whyte, was extensively quoted by the court in its carefully balanced judgment and seemed to provide much of the spine for that ruling (*Reference re. Secession of Quebec* [1998], issued by the Supreme Court on August 20, 1998).

Stéphane Dion was federal intergovernmental affairs minister overseeing this work. Not only did Dion challenge the separatists' stealth strategy in the Supreme Court and ultimately through a law in

Parliament, he directly confronted Quebec Premier Lucien Bouchard in a series of public letters, pointing out the hollowness of the separatist case and the undemocratic dishonesty of their strategy.

Bouchard could not rebut Dion's points. Instead, he cranked up a campaign of personal vilification that went on for many months. Stéphane Dion was labelled as a rat and treated to every insult in the PQ's ethnic nationalist lexicon—but he refused to blink or back down. It was a remarkable performance, the finest moment of Dion's career, and one of the most impressive pieces of work by any federal minister since Justice Minister Pierre Trudeau faced down another populist ethnic nationalist some thirty years before.

I watched Chrétien carefully during that conversation with Romanow. I was struck at how different the prime minister was from his public image. There was none of the 1950s Canadiens hockey player mugging and joking, none of the little guy from Shawinigan. He was cool, smart, thoughtful, well-spoken, in complete command of the complex legal and constitutional files he was discussing with Romanow.

Towards the end of the evening, the business done, the conversation lagged for a moment. I broke protocol and piped up. Why, I asked Chrétien, had he bet so much of his party's political capital in Quebec on Stéphane Dion, as opposed to a more subtle player like Pierre Pettigrew, who might have got the same work done with fewer sparks and less political fallout?

Chrétien very properly seemed surprised at this irrelevant, impertinent question from the wallpaper. Why was wallpaper talking? But then he looked thoughtful for a minute and decided it was an interesting question from a youthful staffer who obviously didn't understand his role, and which could be indulged with an answer (a request to the RCMP security detail to "throw this kid out" was another option he might have been considering).

The separatists' game of repeatedly holding referendums on ambiguous, deceptive questions had to be confronted and ended forever,

Chrétien replied. And that had to be done now, because at some point he was going to retire, and he would likely be replaced by Paul Martin. Martin was too weak, too incapable of making decisions, too eager to curry favour, too gutless to do what had to be done, and so were his friends and supporters. Stéphane Dion, on the other hand, had the determination and backbone to take on Bouchard and to beat him. It was controversial in Quebec's newspapers and television, but the people of Quebec overwhelmingly agreed with Dion and would continue to do so. And once Mr. Dion and the federal government had won, the country would be much less vulnerable to this game.

All of which proved to be true.

Why did any of this matter in 2008?

Because there was a thread of respect for Stéphane Dion in the Western NDP governments that had worked with him when he was federal intergovernmental affairs minister. (He was less of a hit as environment minister under Martin.)

Because a high-profile echo of this had accidentally found its way into a major keynote speech delivered by Jack Layton just before Dion was elected federal Liberal leader.

Because, in the result, the idea of making Dion prime minister seemed less ludicrous to some of us than it seemed (as it turned out) to many other Canadians.

We remembered his record, even if his assault and battery by Conservative attack ads and his foolish decision to run on the Ignatieff tax-shift, carbon-tax issue in the 2008 election had indelibly branded him as a very different kind of leader in the public mind.

It took Layton a while to come around to the views set out above. Layton also remained and remains a sincere critic of Dion's *Clarity Act* strategy as insufficient in itself to reunite and reconcile our country—as is the case. But Layton had an easier time imagining Dion as PM than did most of the public, because of Dion's real record. This provided a small bridge between the two leaders, one on which they could try to build a new, progressive coalition government.

At their meeting that morning, Dion and Layton had discussed the details of how to defeat the Harper government, assuming agreement could be arrived at between the three Opposition parties. The easiest way forward was to defeat the Conservatives on their economic statement. But if the Conservatives suddenly smartened up and withdrew that statement, the two leaders tentatively agreed to take the Conservatives out anyway, through a straight non-confidence motion that the Liberals would table later that day via their upcoming Opposition day motion.

What needed to happen next was a successful bilateral talk with the Liberals, to discuss the shape of the deal and reach agreement on a process to finalize it.

Layton asked me to team up with federal MP Dawn Black, and to lead for the NDP. Our Liberal counterparts would be Liberal house Leader Ralph Goodale and Ottawa public affairs lobbyist Herb Metcalfe.

Dawn Black was perfect for the job Layton was asking her to do. She was a veteran of Ed Broadbent's 1988 caucus, and knew what a winning campaign looked like (the NDP swept British Columbia that year). She represented an urban-suburban riding, and knew what it was like to campaign in the mainstream of Canadian politics. She had tasted defeat, having lost her seat in our 1993 wipeout. She had tasted renewal, returning to Parliament with Layton in 2004. Friendly and easy to work with, she was a feminist strongly committed to economic and social justice and an articulate spokesperson for our party on foreign and military issues. In short, she was a senior, seasoned MP from Western Canada, with a broad grasp of policy and a steady, progressive, mainstream view. She would show her stuff in some notable exchanges that weekend.

We were joined in Layton's office by Ed Broadbent, who reported that Ignatieff and Rae were both planning to be away from Ottawa campaigning in order to keep some distance between themselves and this process. The Liberal caucus would meet Monday. There was a good chance the MPs would address the issue of who should be Liberal leader at that meeting. "It's not likely to be Mr. Dion," Broadbent reported. It could be Rae or it could be someone else. It would most likely be Ignatieff. Broadbent believed there was a "strong push into Monday's meeting from Quebec supporters to get Ignatieff elected."

Layton then called a senior staff meeting to discuss the approach the NDP would take in the bilateral meeting later that day. Layton and McGrath were joined by Broadbent, communications director Brad Lavigne, press secretary Karl Bélanger, executive assistant Ira Dubinsky and me. We sat in a circle in Layton's office.

Discussion ambled around a bit as we got used to the idea that we were about to engage in the details of negotiating a new government. Borrowing a page from Premier Romanow's cabinet-chairing style, I listened to my colleagues without comment for some time, stealing the many ideas that went by and weaving them into the notes I had drawn up that morning about the shape of the deal.

Eventually Layton noticed me hiding in the weeds and asked me to set out how I saw the agreement.

Layton then summed up.

We needed two documents, he decided: a government accord between the NDP and the Liberals and a policy accord between the Liberals, the NDP, and the Bloc. The government accord needed to provide for a proportionate cabinet, by which we meant as many ministers as the NDP would contribute government MPs. The Liberals had 77 MPs while we had 37. We were aiming for one-third of the cabinet. This seemed an issue of fairness and would provide us with a regionally balanced team of experienced NDP ministers that Canadians would be able to imagine running the country, perhaps in a larger role after the next election.

Further, this government accord needed to take us to at least June 2011, allowing the new government to adopt at least two budgets. This spoke to Allan Blakeney's point that, if the coalition were too unstable to survive for long, the short-term controversy about its formation would dominate the subsequent election, not necessarily to our benefit.

The policy accord needed to speak to five points:

- First, the accord should focus on the economic crisis—delivering a major stimulus package.
- Second, the key way to deliver this should be through a broadly defined infrastructure package, including housing, housing retrofits, public transit, and border infrastructure.
- Third, there should be targeted sectoral aid for manufacturing and forestry.
- Fourth, direct help should be provided to the people the NDP was elected to represent—victims of the economic crisis—by enhancing access to employment insurance, and by helping lower-income families by improving the child benefit and child care.
- Fifth, the government should look for common ground with the newly elected Obama administration in the United States by committing to discuss a North American cap-and-trade system to reduce carbon emissions. Layton's theory was that, by framing the NDP's cap-and-trade proposal this way, we would give the Liberals a dignified way to abandon Mr. Ignatieff's tax shift/carbon tax.

By focusing on the economic crisis, we would not have to discuss the NDP's corporate tax proposals or our views on Canada's role in Afghanistan, two issues where we were significantly at odds with the Liberals. This is not to say that we were not going to work on these issues.

Our bet was that the titanic size of the federal deficit in coming years would force the Liberals and any government to reverse Mr. Harper's foolish corporate tax cuts. Events would drive that issue towards us—provided we were in a position to argue the issue at the table at the right time (probably during the second budget).

On Afghanistan, Parliament had voted to withdraw from Canada's military mission in that tragic country by the end of the term we were contemplating for the coalition. So, much more slowly than we would have liked, events would again get us to the result we wanted without an acrimonious debate now with our proposed coalition partner—

provided we were in a position to ensure Parliament's will was enforced without amendment at the time.

Layton directed that this be what we take into our bilateral with the Liberals that afternoon.

Here are a couple of facts that are rarely remarked on.

Whatever else one might think of his government's doings, Prime Minister Brian Mulroney was remarkably effective at the core competencies required of any successful Canadian political leader. Mulroney communicated superbly well with his caucus and his party; he consulted his team carefully; he maintained strong ties of trust and respect with his individual MPs; and he held them together as a team in the face of some of the toughest political challenges ever to face a Canadian federal party. This was a notable achievement for a leader of the federal Progressive Conservative Party, which had a history of suicidal internal division.

One of Prime Minister Mulroney's principal assistants in this work was the honourable member for Lachine–Lac-Saint-Louis, his caucus whip Robert Layton. Jack Layton's father.

I suspect the federal NDP leader disagreed on more than a few policy issues with his Conservative dad, but he clearly had an extremely close family relationship with him, and learned a great deal from him about the critical role of caucus. Layton often reflected on, and referred to, those lessons. He proudly hung Robert Layton's parliamentary certificates next to his own in his office.

Having set his party on the course of these negotiations, having built his bargaining team, and having directed us on what he wanted the agreement to look like and what its policy priorities should be, Layton now turned to what might otherwise have become the trickiest part of the enterprise: keeping the NDP and its family together in support of this initiative.

His first stop was his two deputy leaders, house leader Libby Davies and finance critic Tom Mulcair, then the rest of his caucus executive.

Next came his MPs, individually, followed by several full meetings of caucus (one of which became famous, as I'll note below). Layton consulted leaders and former leaders of the NDP's provincial sections and like-minded city mayors. He spoke carefully to the leaders of the labour movement. He spoke to and BlackBerried his enormous network of other key supporters.

I can't do justice here to the many hours Jack Layton invested into this critical work during the following forty-eight hours, because I was fully occupied with the other tasks he had given me to do. But I can point to the results.

While there were, and remain, sincere and well-founded critics of the coalition project within the NDP, Jack Layton achieved a remarkable level of support within our party for this attempt to give Canada a better government.

That was political leadership at a very high level indeed.

Dawn Black arrived in the leader's office shortly after the staff meeting, and we caught up and compared notes on strategy.

Then we met with a couple of researchers from Layton's office and outlined the policy elements just discussed. We asked them to go through our election platform and other policy work, and flesh out these elements into a point-form first draft our team could work with. This was a daunting job, but we were lucky to have the right people. Emily Watkins is a bright, sharp, deceptively soft-spoken woman, who was coming to assume a key role in Jack Layton's office as it moved slowly to convert the additional funding earned by our larger caucus into a rebirth of "NDP Research," our much-missed federal-policy-and-research shop. Ian Wayne contributed to our 2008 platform. They undertook to review the state-of-play of our policy work, with a view to producing a workable three-to-five-page summary we could work from in negotiations with the Liberals.

Our first exploratory meeting with the Liberals began in mid-afternoon that day in an airless boardroom on the second floor of the Sheraton Hotel in downtown Ottawa. Liberal house Leader Ralph Goodale and Ottawa policy consultant Herb Metcalfe led the Liberal team.

I had never met Metcalfe before and knew nothing about him. I soon found him to be a smart, friendly, thoughtful political advisor, who was working with remarkable commitment to try to get his luckless leader back on a winning track.

Mr. Goodale, on the other hand, I knew quite a bit about. I was mostly pleased that the Liberal Party's lone Saskatchewan MP was going to play such a key role in these discussions, with a little undertone of worry.

I was pleased because, as I noted above, we had put some thought earlier in the game into proposing that Mr. Goodale be named prime minister of the coalition government.

Further, Allan Blakeney was going to be a key part of our team that weekend. Goodale and Blakeney had known each other in the Saskatchewan legislature—Blakeney as Opposition leader, Goodale as leader and sole MLA for the Saskatchewan provincial Liberals. In the 1986 provincial election, Goodale had waged a lonely campaign on a platform of strict fiscal discipline, while the Progressive Conservatives and the NDP duelled over how much more could be done by government for the economy and public services. Goodale had been clobbered in that election. But he turned out to be right about the fiscal state of the province. When Premier Romanow was elected in 1991 and found himself confronted with the disastrous fiscal mess left by the Conservatives, our government tackled the issues Goodale had been trying to warn about in 1986. In that sense, there was some hope for finding a common fiscal language with Goodale.

On the other hand, Mr. Goodale worried me, because he had cause not to love our party.

In 2005, he was Paul Martin's finance minister. He was well and justly respected by all parties in Parliament as a scrupulously honest, competent, and careful fiscal manager. But he could not help Prime

Minister Martin find a coherent narrative for his government or to avoid defeat—bedevilled as Martin's team was by the "sponsorship scandal" and many other burdens.

So Mr. Goodale could be forgiven for wanting to avoid further trouble when it became clear, in November 2005, on the eve of the Martin government's defeat, that someone in his department had leaked details of an announcement Goodale made that month about income trusts. It was evident, from a series of unusual trades, that players on Bay Street had foreknowledge of the finance minister's announcement. But in an angry press conference, Goodale denied that anyone on his staff or in his department had leaked anything. Mr. Goodale was unwise to be so categorical about this, since he could not be sure of the conduct of every individual in his department.

This was certainly the view of Elliot Anderson, perhaps our party's most effective political researcher. Anderson, director of research of our Ontario NDP caucus in Queen's Park at the time, was on leave and working in the "pit" of the federal NDP war room, reporting to war-room unit director Ray Guardia, who in return reported to me as NDP national campaign director. At the time, we were a week into setting up our 2006 campaign organization.

Anderson watched Goodale's press conference, and proposed to Guardia that, since the minister was refusing to look into an obvious leak from his department, perhaps we should up the ante and call on the RCMP commercial-crimes unit to investigate the matter for him.

As it happened, both Guardia and I had some previous experience with the RCMP in roughly similar circumstances.

During the 1988 federal election, as I noted above, I was the NDP campaign chair in the Quebec riding of Chambly, while Guardia was the campaign manager. One day, our campaign received a thick brown envelope giving us a detailed report on some interesting activities by our sitting Conservative opponent, Progressive Conservative MP Richard Grisé. According to our informant, a member of Mr. Grisé's staff, Mr.

Grisé was part of a network running an organized kickback scheme in Quebec, which was skimming federal contracts. We tried to interest the Montreal *Gazette*, the CBC, Radio-Canada, *La Presse*, and *Le Devoir* in this revelation. None agreed to look into it unless there was some third-party validation—such as, for example, an RCMP investigation. So we contacted the RCMP, provided them with the envelope, and asked them to look into it.

The RCMP replied, in as many words, that the RCMP would not involve itself in a federal election and would do nothing about the information at that time.

It was subsequently revealed, as the federal Commission for Public Complaints Against the RCMP put it discreetly in a later report, that "then Prime Minister Brian Mulroney's principal secretary had sent a letter to the RCMP discussing the allegations against Mr. Grisé less than two weeks prior to the election."

On election day, Grisé defeated our candidate.

The day after the election, the RCMP executed a search warrant in Grisé's office, carting away his files. Grisé was subsequently charged with fraud and corruption. He pleaded guilty on the first day of his trial, and was sentenced to a day in jail, three years' probation, and a $20,000 fine.

It's too bad that Mr. Grisé pleaded guilty. The public was denied a detailed inquiry into exactly what Mr. Grisé had been up to, and who else might have been involved.

Our candidate, Phil Edmonston, who ran in the subsequent by-election and won a crushing victory, was not pleased that the RCMP had refused to act on a well-substantiated complaint for political reasons, and called on RCMP Commissioner Norman Inkster to resign (which he respectfully declined to do).

So, eighteen years later, here we were again.

Guardia and I were more than skeptical that the RCMP would do anything about the obvious income-trust leak. But, in part to gently poke our friends on the force about how they had handled Mr. Grisé's case, we asked Anderson to work up a letter with NDP finance critic Judy Wasylycia-Leis asking, once again, for an investigation.

The RCMP Complaints Commission summarized what happened next:

> *On December 23, 2005, Commissioner Zaccardelli faxed Ms. Wasylycia-Leis a letter stating that the matter that she raised had been reviewed, and that the RCMP would be commencing a criminal investigation. On December 28, 2005, Ms. Wasylycia-Leis posted the Commissioner's letter on her website and the NDP issued a press release concerning the letter. In the evening of December 28, 2005, the RCMP issued its own press release stating that the RCMP was undertaking a criminal investigation into the matter. The RCMP's press release stated that there was no evidence of wrongdoing or illegal activity on the part of those associated to the investigation, including Mr. Goodale.*

We were astonished. This time the media had their third-party validation in spades.

This proved unhelpful to Mr. Martin and his campaign. Liberal support in election tracking polls dropped significantly after these revelations, and did not recover.

Further, as with Mr. Grisé, there was something to the case, or at least enough to lead to a criminal charge. On February 14, 2007, Serge Nadeau, a director general in the Finance Department's tax-policy unit, was charged for offences related to Mr. Goodale's trust announcement.

This being so, Mr. Goodale would have been better advised to say that he was concerned about the unusual activity in the market, had ordered an internal investigation, and would report to Parliament when he had all the facts. That would have been the end of the matter. Perhaps the Martin government might then have been re-elected.

Mr. Goodale was understandably bitter about these events. In the world of political campaigning (fought in eight-word sound bites) some voters were left with the impression that Mr. Goodale himself might have done something wrong. That was clearly not the case. Mr. Goodale is faultlessly honest. He simply took some poor advice from some official or political staffer, in giving a blanket defence of his department in the face of clear evidence that a leak had occurred.

And now there he was that afternoon, sitting in front of me, about to discuss a coalition government with the federal NDP. As it turned out, thankfully, Goodale never raised this matter, but I suspect it was on his mind. I am a little sorry that I never had a chance during these discussions to apologize to him for any suggestion his own integrity was an issue.

Here is that apology now, Mr. Goodale.

We got down to business. After some conversational throat-clearing about the weather and a round of introductions, Herb Metcalfe opened the discussion by saying that the Liberals were committed to trying to negotiate a coalition, and wanted to get that coalition's key principles down on paper as quickly as possible. "We need to have a letter signed by Monday," Metcalfe said. "A letter from Jack, Duceppe, and Dion to the governor general."

I agreed to this proposal—we would sign a joint letter from the entire Opposition to the governor general, telling her that a majority of Parliament supported a new government.

I then suggested we talk in more detail about the "shape of the deal." When Metcalfe agreed, I outlined our view, reading from the notes I had taken of Jack Layton's direction a few hours before.

We proposed that we work up two documents: a government accord between the Liberals and the NDP and a policy accord that would also have the support of the Bloc. The government accord between the Liberals and the NDP would provide for a coalition, a proportionate cabinet, and a term running until June 2011 to permit two budgets. The policy accord would commit the new government to a focus on the economic crisis. There would be a stimulus package, including infrastructure investment; income support and security; and co-operation with the Obama administration on priorities like a continental environmental cap-and-trade system.

If this was roughly the shape of the deal we were both interested in, Dawn Black and I suggested we discuss the government accord on Saturday with a view to negotiating it in final form, and then that we discuss the policy accord Sunday. We proposed this work plan because we had a fairly clear idea about what we wanted in the government accord, but we needed more time to do our homework on the policy issues. The agenda we outlined created a workday on Saturday that our mother ship could use to carefully consider those policy issues.

Metcalfe and Goodale agreed to this work plan.

Goodale discussed some of the parliamentary issues around defeating the Conservatives. The Liberals would table several draft Opposition day motions immediately. There were several motions we could choose from, he said. One would be a straight non-confidence motion. This might then set up two separate votes Monday on which the government could be defeated—the ways-and-means motion and the Liberal confidence motion.

Metcalfe talked about the press. He proposed that we adopt a joint communications approach, and say as little as possible to journalists while we were working. "It's best for all of us if much is left to idle speculation," he pointed out.

Things seemed to be going well. The discussion was also drifting into operating issues of secondary importance. So it was time to test how solid this house was by delving into some of the tougher questions.

"Let's talk about who is going to be prime minister," I said. "Who you have as your leader is entirely up to you. We'll work with whomever the Liberal Party chooses. But since Mr. Dion has resigned, and in the spirit of 'idle speculation,' who do you think will be your designate for prime minister?"

There were some interesting expressions on faces of the Liberal team members when I asked this question. Metcalfe answered.

"You'd have to be stupid to not use the current leader," he said. "How could we possibly pass up this opportunity? But some people might take a contrary view. The leader is calling some of the caucus members who are supporters of his. We need to arrive at a deal. If we get there, then we can get our internal matters cleared up."

There was a longish silence in the room while Dawn Black and I digested this answer. What Metcalfe was telling us was that Mr. Dion intended to use a coalition accord to "unresign"—to step back into the Liberal leadership as prime minister of a new government, much as Pierre Trudeau did in 1979 after the fall of the Clark government. This explained the determination of Dion's negotiators to have the accord wrapped up by Monday, when their leader would have to face his caucus.

What were our interests?

In the very short term, the Liberals had just handed us some serious leverage in these negotiations. The coalition was a do-or-die proposition for their leader. That meant they probably weren't going to walk away, provided the accord was in a form they could get through their caucus.

But in the bigger picture, we were indelibly weaving the coalition into the fate of Mr. Dion, unless we moved immediately to change the game. If Mr. Dion was going to use the coalition to keep his job, that meant Mr. Ignatieff might end up opposing the coalition for the same reason, and Ignatieff's people believed he had over fifty MPs in his corner.

A bolder, perhaps more effective, approach might have been to stop the talks at that moment, and to tell the Liberals that we could not proceed until we knew who the Liberal leader was. This might have handed us Ignatieff to deal with that Monday—who, perhaps, would have proceeded with this project in his new circumstances. But none of the signals from his camp were encouraging, which is why we stuck with the Liberal we knew. Dion was the leader. It was Dion with whom we had to deal. Liberal leadership politics were too dark and murky for

FRIDAY, NOVEMBER 28, 2008

us to try to navigate them. We would have to take our chances, and see what happened.

It was time to break the silence and ask more interesting questions. "What are your plans with regard to senior appointments and ABCs [agencies, boards, and commissions]?" I asked.

Metcalfe answered that, in their view, there didn't need to be wholesale changes to the senior public service. But there were definitely five or six deputy ministers—he cited the deputy minister of finance—who were not going to be comfortable with the new agenda and would need to be moved. They didn't have any particular thoughts on ABCs. I offered that some of the federal government's boards (I cited the Canadian International Trade Tribunal and the CRTC) were of particular interest to us, and that we would be proposing some language on Saturday that respected the prime minister's prerogatives but contemplated consultation on the composition of boards.

Metcalfe raised the size of the cabinet. Mr. Dion was interested in a much smaller cabinet than Harper had, he said. They would be looking at twenty-four ministers. Reducing the cabinet would save the government much of the $16 million or so that Harper was trying to claw back from public financing of political parties. I said that sounded quite acceptable. This point offered an opportunity for us to get into the relative share of cabinet between the two parties. I told Metcalfe we would be looking for the cabinet to be proportional to the relative weight of our caucuses. This didn't seem to surprise either Metcalfe or Goodale, and they noted it down without demur.

Metcalfe moved on to what seemed to be a favourite topic of his, the need for a minister whose sole job would be to oversee cabinet committees and to ensure they all really worked. We received this proposal without comment.

At this point, I proposed that we review our notes and make sure we had clearly heard each other on the "shape of the deal." I went through the deal points again: an NDP–Liberal governing coalition; a policy accord also supported by the Bloc; a proportional cabinet; a two-and-a-half-year mandate to June 2011; a focus on the economy. They agreed that this was the shape of the deal.

Goodale outlined his proposal for a thirty-day consultation process about the economy and the next budget. He said what needed to be done was fairly clear, but that there should be a wide consultation process to ensure stakeholders were heard and the government's actions were seen to be legitimate and based on wide agreement.

I pointed out that the stimulus package we were contemplating, plus the corporate tax cuts that the Liberals favoured, were going to add up to a very substantial deficit, and I asked Goodale if he was comfortable with that. Goodale replied that our goal had to be to get back on track to debt reduction as quickly as possible after the economic crisis was over, aiming for a goal of having the debt down to 20 per cent of GDP by 2020. The recovery plan would have to include some suggestion of how to get the federal government back to fiscal health.

We thought that was fine, betting it could not be achieved without backing off on the corporate tax cuts Harper introduced and the Liberals supported.

"Do you expect the agenda to include your carbon-tax proposal?" I asked next. Everyone laughed. No, they didn't. A continental cap-and-trade system was the way to go. The two programs were basically equivalent if carefully costed out and would get us to the same end. There was no talk of a "tax shift" anymore. Agreed.

Goodale went directly to the corporate tax issue. Did we understand that some of those measures were needed? I said we would see, as the government's fiscal strategy played itself out.

Metcalfe raised the final issue that day: dispute resolution. If we were going to persuade the governor general that we had a viable government, we needed some sort of machinery to resolve disputes among the coalition partners, short of having the government come apart. The Liberals were thinking of some sort of party elders' committee, to which we could refer disputes for mediation. Since Broadbent and Chrétien seemed to be working well together behind the scenes, this sounded like a good idea to us. We agreed, suggesting that Chrétien and similar figures from the Liberal Party could be their picks, and that people like Ed Broadbent, Allan Blakeney, and Roy Romanow would figure among ours.

Both sides thought we had enough to report back to our principals. Metcalfe said the Liberals had reserved the penthouse boardroom on the seventeenth floor of the same hotel for the following day. We agreed we would consult the people we worked for. If they were satisfied with progress, we'd resume then.

Dawn Black and I stumped back to Layton's caucus services office a few blocks from the hotel, doing a debrief en route. We marvelled at the role of Liberal leadership politics in this affair. This was about Mr. Dion retracting his resignation, pushing Ignatieff and Rae back into the ranks, and grabbing the prime ministership. The audacity of what he was trying to do kind of impressed us. And worried us.

We reported progress to Layton. He felt things were on track and that the negotiations should continue. At Layton's direction I e-mailed Metcalfe (5:54 p.m.): "Confirming for 10:00 a.m. tomorrow." The Liberal negotiator was succinct in reply (6:05 p.m.): "See you at 10:00 a.m."

Meanwhile, the government was waking up. For good or ill we had clearly telegraphed what we were going to do, and the cable news programs had been full of well-informed speculation throughout our meeting—although they never found out where we were.

A little after 6:00 p.m., Prime Minister Harper made a statement in the foyer of the House of Commons. He launched an effective, well-crafted political attack on the coalition proposal. "While we have been working on the economy, the Opposition has been working on a backroom deal to overturn the results of the last election without seeking the consent of voters. They want to take power, not earn it," Harper said. "The Liberals campaigned against a coalition with the NDP, saying NDP policies were bad for the economy. And now they want to form a coalition, saying that this will strengthen the economy."

The prime minister then pulled a rabbit out of his hat. Using the government's prerogative in the house, he announced that both the Liberal Opposition day and the government ways-and-means motion would be delayed a week, to December 8. This bought the Conservatives time to consider their options, to allow tempers to cool on the Opposition benches—and, they could hope, for the Liberal leadership crisis to strangle Dion and bring forward a new Liberal leader who might be more helpful to the Conservative government.

Ignatieff was the key risk. The contact in Ignatieff's camp, with whom I had been BlackBerrying on the tarmac that morning (seemingly a year ago) had predicted the prime minister's language. I decided to use this as a peg to take the temperature of the Ignatieff camp.

"Interesting moves by Harper," I BlackBerried him at 6:47 p.m. "You predicted his lines pretty accurately."

"Calgary DNA," my friend replied (6:48 p.m.). "Still looked like a guy applying for his own job."

It was time to try a little business. I replied (6:49 p.m.): "He looked upset and worried to me. Are your folks any more comfortable with what your folks are doing?"

His reply (6:51 p.m.): "Nope. We may not let him do it. Stay tuned."

That didn't sound helpful. I replied (6:52 p.m.): "Pity. Good opportunity."

Back at me (6:53 p.m.): "That's a matter of perspective."

I mused about this for a few minutes. At 6:57 p.m. I texted: "I suggest you check instincts with your old PM before locking: he's got a pretty good perspective." I was challenging my correspondent to speak to Jean Chrétien.

This didn't turn out to be the trump card I was hoping for in this exchange. He replied (within a minute, 6:57 p.m.): "Already did. Instincts don't equal caucus."

I asked (6:58 p.m.): "Can we help?" Which drew no reply.

It seemed this project was in trouble in the Liberal caucus. There wasn't much we could do about it except to try to speak to as many Liberals as possible, and try to persuade them we were fit partners and that the coalition was a good idea. This was heavy sledding, since our contacts with the Liberals were so poor.

So, it was time to get in touch with Bob Rae's team.

I first met Bob Rae in 1981 in the student-union building of McGill University. I was a young writer for the *McGill Daily*. He was a slightly-less-young finance critic and MP in the federal NDP caucus, on a speaking tour with Ed Broadbent. Broadbent gave an impressive speech to a roomful of students. After that, Rae took the floor and outlined his proposals for addressing the recession then on the horizon. Rae's basic idea was that Canada should impose tight exchange controls, which would in turn allow the Bank of Canada to reduce interest rates.

I interviewed Rae after the speech. Summoning every ounce of the insufferability available to young student journalists on the *McGill Daily*, my first question went something like this: "How would you respond to those who argue that, in this age of massive foreign investment, electronic transfers, and other new ways to move money around, exchange controls are an outdated and stupid idea?" Rae quite correctly blew his stack at this disrespectful question. I remember Broadbent watching his answer with the slightest crooked smile.

I didn't get to ask another question.

By the time of the 1989 Chambly by-election to replace Mr. Grisé, Bob Rae was leader of the Ontario NDP and architect of an accord with the Peterson Liberals that had finally unseated the Ontario Progressive Conservatives. He was leader of the official Opposition, and a few months away from the premiership. Very few of the (generally unilingual French-speaking) residents of St-Bruno, Ste-Amable, and the other communities making up the riding of Chambly had ever heard of Bob Rae. But the NDP staff on the campaign certainly had. Bob Rae was a hero to us all. We were keen to have him come to help with our campaign, basically because we wanted to meet him.

The fluently bilingual Rae had long been a friend of the Quebec section of the NDP, and he graciously accepted our request to give us a day canvassing with our candidate. Unfortunately, the young student we sent to pick him up at the airport couldn't find our campaign office. And so, after a very long wait, our candidate hit the road to do his small-town canvassing. Most of the campaign staff left with him or checked out to have lunch. Eventually, the office was empty except for me, campaign manager Guardia, and George Nakitsas, Ed Broadbent's chief of staff, there to give advice and help with fundraising.

Just as we were locking up and heading out to the local Chinese–Greek restaurant (an interesting establishment) to talk a little fundraising business, a very red-faced student deposited a very red-faced Bob Rae and fled. There wasn't much we could do, since our candidate was long gone, and in this pre-cellphone era we had no way to track him down. So we invited Rae to join us for a nice Chinese–Greek lunch.

Rae sat silently through our meal and fundraising discussion. Then he put up his hand.

"I just want to say one thing," he said. He had our attention. "When I was a young man, if this had happened, I would have said" . . . he raised his voice . . . "What the *fuck* are you guys doing *wasting my time* when I have *serious work to do* . . ." It continued in this vein for some time. Then he stopped, paused, and said in a perfectly calm voice: "But I'm mature now, and I won't do that."

I had seen him as a young man. We were impressed.

The next time I met Bob Rae was in 1995. The Romanow team was heavily focused on preparations for a Saskatchewan provincial election. My work was all about our message—putting together an election platform; thinking about tour issues; and planning our election speechwriting, media, research, and tour units. I was slated to run the Saskatchewan NDP campaign war room.

David Mackenzie, a leader in the national staff of the United Steelworkers, son of Ontario NDP Labour minister Bob Mackenzie, had a roughly similar mandate in Rae's leader's office. But Mackenzie's team was in a fundamentally different position than we were. We were going into the 1995 election comfortably ahead of our Liberal and Conservative opponents. The Ontario NDP was (depending on the poll) twenty to thirty points behind. Mackenzie had an extremely difficult job, made worse by many of his colleagues. They had given up and seemed to be of a mind to run a campaign under the slogan "Let's Get This Over With" (better than "The Land Is Strong," but not by much).

But Mackenzie refused to give up, and tried to put together a campaign, preferably a winning campaign.

As part of that effort, he invited Saskatchewan NDP chief of staff Garry Aldridge and me to give seminars to his team on what we were up to. We talked to them about how we were positioning ourselves electorally, and described the campaign we were putting together. Half of the Ontario NDP staff we spoke to seemed bright, young, eager. Half seemed prematurely aged, crushed, bitter, and dismissive of what we were saying. It appeared that Rae's leader's office was in the midst of a sort of civil war over whether there was anything they could do about their lot.

I was brought in to meet Premier Rae. He gave me one minute, thanked me politely for coming in to visit his team, and over and out. A former backbench MPP in Rae's government caucus told me recently that most of their meetings with the premier were like that, too.

Finally, I met Bob Rae for breakfast in the company of Roy Romanow in early 2005. I had been waging a campaign for some time to convince Premier Romanow (who had stepped down from the Saskatchewan legislative assembly in February 2001) to run for the federal Parliament as a Saskatoon federal NDP candidate. Many people have tried to convince Romanow to run for Parliament. Perhaps I got closer than some. But he was not inclined to step into a federal NDP caucus by himself. In the unlikely event he decided he wanted to leave his beloved hometown and enter Parliament as a federal NDP MP, he wanted to go as part of a team that would drive a fundamental economic and political rethink in the party, change its profile on fiscal issues, and hopefully help it make the jump into office.

Romanow and Rae had spoken about getting involved in federal politics together a number of times in the past. Now, Romanow proposed that Rae consider joining him as a federal NDP candidate in the 2006 election, so that the two could work together to drive change in "the family."

Rae replied that the NDP was not his family, and that he would never consider doing such a thing, not in a million years. The NDP was no longer his party, Rae told us. He then abruptly walked out on our breakfast.

There was much that underlay that answer.

Rae had recently repudiated his federal NDP affiliation, saying he could no longer stomach the anti-Israeli public statements of NDP foreign affairs critic Svend Robinson, who Rae described as a "histrionic crank." Since the federal NDP was allowing Robinson to speak for it in an over-the-top, wildly unbalanced way about critical issues in the Middle East, Rae turned his back on the party.

The Ontario NDP for its part turned its back on him. They refused to elect his preferred candidate to succeed him and distanced itself from him politically. His photo was removed from their caucus room and the NDP caucus refused to applaud him when he was introduced in the Ontario legislature by Liberal Premier Dalton McGuinty (Rae having authored a report for the Liberal government on post-secondary education that the NDP rejected). Words were not minced when Rae returned to the Liberal Party.

If only.

If only Rae and his team had better controlled and explained their budget during their first year in office; had brought in a compelling "signature achievement" like public auto insurance; had traded Premier Rae's loyal support for the Meech Lake and Charlottetown accords for a better fiscal deal for Ontario from Mulroney; and had used the tools available to government to control spending without asking public-sector unions to voluntarily roll back their compensation in mid-contract. If only Rae had been able, in short, to compile a record of which the party could be prouder—thus avoiding the bitter post-government splits in our Ontario section.

If only the Ontario NDP and its sole former premier had been able to maintain an appropriate relationship (former leaders and premiers are revered in the Saskatchewan CCF–NDP. Among many benefits, this keeps them on the team).

If only the federal NDP had fielded a sensible foreign affairs critic in the early part of this decade—one in touch with both the moderate liberation voices of Palestine and the responsible left in Israel.

And if only Romanow and Rae had been able and willing to make something of Romanow's casual proposal that day. Jack Layton and the federal NDP would then have added some serious bench strength to what was already a formidable caucus. The NDP would have had less ground to make up as a credible governing party. Perhaps Jack Layton's coalition proposal would therefore have been a less fragile proposition. And as a result, perhaps Canada at this writing would be governed by a progressive cabinet fit to address the economic crisis grinding it.

Rae, of course, instead joined the Liberals and simultaneously announced he was running for the Liberal leadership. One of Rae's senior NDP cabinet ministers cried when he heard Rae had done this. Many New Democrats agreed that it would be a good thing to make Bob Rae cry, too.

As a guest at the December 2006 Liberal leadership convention, I arranged to be standing in a good spot and took a photo of Rae's face the moment he released his delegates, having lost the Liberal leadership race. He wasn't crying, but it would do.

Things change.

In politics, to steal an old phrase, parties hoping to prevail admit to no permanent alliances or enmities, but they do pursue permanent interests. We were trying to put together a coalition with the Liberals in pursuit of a permanent interest: getting into office, so that we could implement some of our agenda. Rae was once again running for the Liberal leadership. His principal opponent's team was making it clear they didn't love the coalition proposal. We needed to see if we could grow the number of voices inside the Liberal caucus who were comfortable with the idea of joining us in government. It was therefore time for the federal NDP, including me, to get over our feelings about Bob Rae and to see if he might be an objective ally in pursuing these interests.

That night, working through several intermediaries, I contacted the Rae camp. It didn't take long to hear from Rae's key organizers. They let us know that they were completely excluded from the negotiations and were hopping mad about it. They wanted us to understand that in no way were Mr. Dion and his team representing the Rae campaign.

That said, as Friday evening unfolded and discussions continued, they gave us to understand that Bob Rae himself had been carefully considering the issue, and was increasingly leaning towards supporting the coalition proposal. Better, he was starting to think about what could be done within the Liberal caucus to make it work. Specifically, Rae was thinking about meeting with Ignatieff and Dominic Leblanc, his two main opponents in the Liberal leadership race.

As a small contribution towards making this a more comfortable thing for Rae to do, I offered his team the novelty of some civil talk from the NDP. By late Friday night, I was harbouring the hope that Rae would help Dion promote the coalition inside the Liberal caucus. Perhaps that would give his university roommate, Mr. Ignatieff, cause to reconsider.

There were two big pieces of work left to tackle that Friday night, in addition to seeing what we could do within our extremely limited means to nudge the furniture in the Liberal caucus. We needed to get our policy proposals in order so that they could be carefully reviewed by our core working team the following day. And we needed to have a very clear idea about what we wanted in a government accord with the Liberals—the topic of negotiations in a few hours.

Anne McGrath and I met with Emily Watkins and Ian Wayne. They had done a good job of combing our policy material, and had produced a lengthy memorandum with numerous detailed policy proposals much loved by New Democrat candidates in the recent election, with costings. It was an excellent start.

I pulled out a pen and drew lines through perhaps 70 per cent of this work, knowing that each detail was an additional bargaining point, and that we would not have time to do more than agree on key directions and priorities when the time came to discuss the policy accord with the Liberals and then with the Bloc. Our list needed to stick closely to the tight agenda outlined by our federal leader. Watkins and Wayne gamely undertook to go into rewrite. Their deadline was 10:00 a.m. Saturday morning, when they would have to present their ideas to Allan Blakeney, Ed Broadbent, and Jack Layton.

McGrath and I then met in her office with Broadbent and with Blakeney, who had just arrived from a difficult-as-always flight from Saskatoon via Air Canada. We briefed them on the discussions with the Liberals that day, and outlined what we had discussed in Layton's office earlier about the "shape of the deal" and how we might try to land the agreement that weekend. Both carefully reviewed each point, probing and challenging the many uncertainties and risks, weighing the alternatives. It is a formidable thing to be reporting simultaneously to Allan Blakeney and Ed Broadbent. I thought it was great fun, and a great privilege. This done, they agreed to lead the review of our policy proposals the following day with Layton, and to join the negotiations Sunday for the tricky policy discussion.

At 7:28 p.m. Kathleen Monk, our deputy communications director, circulated a research note that confirmed the government was within its rights to defer a vote on both its own ways-and-means motion and the Liberal Opposition day. We had been looking into ways to overrule the prime minister on this point, but we were going to have to concede that Mr. Harper had bought himself a week.

I needed to get out of the office. I had clear direction from Layton, Blakeney, Broadbent, and McGrath on the government accord. Now I needed to go and hide in my hotel room to digest our discussions and commit them to paper, and I needed to consult the only senior New Democrat who had ever pulled off such an accord—Roy Romanow.

I got him on the phone at about 11:00 p.m. Ottawa time. Romanow had been following the news stories closely and had been speaking to some of the players that day, including Mr. Chrétien and Jack Layton.

I summarized the state-of-play as I saw it, and how we proposed to handle the negotiations that weekend. Romanow listened patiently and then cut right to a key point: who is going to be the prime minister in this coalition government, given that Mr. Dion has resigned? I told him what we knew about the coming Monday Liberal caucus meeting, about Mr. Dion's hope to "unresign," about the signals from Ignatieff's camp that they might remove Mr. Dion and supplant him.

Romanow wondered if the best interim prime minister might not be Jean Chrétien himself. Chrétien could serve as an effective "bridger" on the Liberal team. The majority who seemed to want Dion out would get their wish, Ignatieff and Rae could focus on competing for leader, and Mr. Chrétien could pilot the new government for an interim period, as a PM both the Liberals and the NDP could work with comfortably.

It was an excellent idea, but there was nothing we could do to make it happen. Given Ignatieff's apparent power in the Liberal caucus, it seemed more likely that a leadership change would produce Ignatieff as the new PM, with Rae and Dion getting "big jobs."

This has got to work," Romanow told me. "The chemistry between the various leaders, and between them and Layton, is important." He was reflecting here on the key ace he held when his own time had come to negotiate a coalition with Liberals. In 1999, he had an excellent personal relationship with Liberal leader Melenchuk, a relationship that grew into real trust and respect during the Saskatchewan coalition. There needed to be similar bonds of trust to make this coalition work. I reflected ruefully on the almost total lack of contact between any of the Liberal players and our team.

Romanow thought the coalition proposal was going to come under brutal attack from the Conservatives in the media in coming days. The basic case for the coalition needed to be set out. Perhaps, he suggested, there should be an op-ed piece jointly drafted by Chrétien and Broadbent.

One of Romanow's principal worries was how the role of the Bloc was going to play in Western Canada. They might well turn out to be political poison, he said.

And, of course, he turned out to be right.

He noted that CBC's *The National* was spinning against the coalition, raising uncertainty by reporting that we might demand an "NDP finance minister." We agreed that, given the flavour still lingering in Eastern Canada about NDP government, this rumour should be addressed directly during negotiations the following day.

We talked through the key elements of the Saskatchewan coalition that looked applicable. I began by asking him to walk me through how we had organized the NDP and Liberal caucuses during the Saskatchewan coalition. He confirmed that we had agreed to maintain two separate and distinct caucuses on the government benches, although in practice the Liberal ministers tended to attend the NDP caucus as well, and a common conversation about the government quickly developed.

"These agreements need to be ratified by the executives of our respective parties," Romanow said. "It's critical to get the parties on board, with motions on file."

Here again he was reflecting on his experience. While the Saskatchewan NDP and Liberal caucuses quickly settled into an excellent working relationship, Liberal leader Melenchuk was never able to achieve peace with the many critics on his party executive who opposed the arrangement. Over the following months, the Saskatchewan Liberal party imploded as a result.

I asked Romanow to review the rules governing his coalition cabinet. He went through the core rules of confidentiality and solidarity that make cabinet government possible, and urged that these be carried into the federal coalition.

I described a phrase I had seen in New Zealand coalition accords that I thought might serve very well: "no surprises." I suggested the two parties explicitly commit to a "no surprises" approach to working together. The NDP would be a principal beneficiary of such a rule, since so much in government happens in the central agencies (Prime Minister's Office, Privy Council Office, Finance) over which we would have no control. A "no surprises" policy would give us a tool to demand transparency and consultation. The Liberals for their part could hope, through this arrangement, for a minimum of freelancing by their coalition partner. Romanow thought it was a useful idea. At the end of the day it comes down to the chemistry between the players, he said. He met with Melenchuk a great deal. "He was not an enemy, but I held him very close," Romanow said. This approach wasn't written into the Saskatchewan accord but was a fundamental part of it.

I asked Romanow to tell me how "ABC" appointments (appointments to agencies, boards, and commissions) worked in the Saskatchewan coalition. He said the Liberals were only consulted about these in their own ministries, and never sought input on other appointments. Nonetheless, Romanow recalled, he consulted Melenchuk on his own initiative on a number of tricky appointments, because he came to view the Liberal leader as a good advisor. I thought we would want a larger role than this on federal appointments, especially key ones, but Romanow pointed out that key appointments like the naming of deputy ministers are central to the prime minister's prerogatives, and that this must not be undermined if the government was going to function. The principle in our government was that the deputy ministers worked for the premier, and the federal system was likely similar. So be it, but in my view the NDP needed to put down a clear marker that, at least on key appointments—Supreme Court Justices, the CRTC—we would expect to be consulted. Grudgingly, Romanow allowed that this would be fine.

I noted that over thirty Senate appointments would be available to the government in the next two years.

"What advantage is there to those appointments?" Romanow asked. "In their current form they're nothing but partisan rewards. No point worrying about it unless, late in its mandate, the new government has an appetite to tackle moving to an elected Senate. Why would anyone want to be a Senator now? Make it a true bicameral legislature, and maybe people would be interested."

Romanow raised an issue close to his heart. The new government needed to take a strong position in favour of defending the federal spending power, a power the Conservatives were constantly threatening to undermine.

"The current government is committed to non-activity," he said. "They are committed to non-activity on the economy, on social issues, and on fiscal issues. In the long term, if this continues, provincial governments will inevitably fill the void, with Ottawa's implicit forbearance. If we want social programs that are roughly equivalent from sea to sea, the federal spending power needs to be used, it needs to be protected, and it needs to be explained." (Layton and his caucus would have agreed, with an "asymmetrical" exception in Quebec.)

Finally, Romanow raised the issue of a dispute settlement mechanism. This was going to be a tricky proposition, he said, especially in a politically charged situation. For example, what would happen if an NDP minister "got into trouble" and a Liberal prime minister felt the need to remove that minister? I outlined Herb Metcalfe's proposal for a dispute settlement mechanism driven by "wise people," and asked Romanow if he would be willing to serve on such a committee himself. He agreed.

We had what we needed. Working from my notes and fresh from my conversation with Romanow, I outlined an opening throw on the shape of a coalition agreement with the Liberals. It was late and it was high time to go to bed, but I was wide awake and wired. So I turned my pen to one last bit of business. I scrawled out a draft letter to the governor general, intended to be signed by Dion, Layton, and Duceppe, setting out why Parliament had lost confidence in Harper, asserting that the majority supported a new ministry, and stating that the new team was ready to take office. The Liberals had proposed this. We'd give them a draft.

Saturday,
November 29, 2008

A T 10:00 A.M., ALLAN BLAKENEY, ED BROADBENT, AND JACK Layton settled down with a staff team in a windowless boardroom in the NDP caucus office to review, discuss, and debate the policy proposals we would put to the Liberals. This meeting would be followed later that day by a caucus meeting to consult our MPs.

Dawn Black and I headed up to the penthouse boardroom at the Sheraton Hotel.

Herb Metcalfe continued to lead for the Liberals, but he showed up with a new team—Marlene Jennings, a Liberal MP from an anglophone riding in Montreal and Liberal deputy house leader (standing in for Goodale, absent that day); Dion's chief of staff, Johanne Sénécal; and Dion's deputy chief of staff, Katie Telford.

Since we were now outnumbered two to one, we briefly considered calling for two more New Democrats to round out our team. In the end, we decided not to, reasoning that having a smaller team might turn out to be an advantage, as indeed it did.

We began by talking about Metcalfe's proposal that the three parties send a letter to the governor general. We offered our draft, which was reviewed and quickly agreed to with little substantive amendment. A little too quickly, I thought.

In other negotiations, I've seen periods when it seemed that the union could make no proposal that the employer wouldn't accept. At ACTRA we've called this the "collecting the flowers" phase. Almost without fail, what was going on was that the employer had a bomb they were planning to drop, and they were trying to accumulate some positive capital, create some goodwill, and generate some momentum in the talks before getting to the tough stuff. In my view this tactic doesn't work, but from the union's perspective it is a pleasant period in a negotiation, because much of what you might like to get, you get. Before the anvil drops.

Sénécal left the meeting.

We turned to the main piece of business before us: the government accord. I told Metcalfe that we had been thinking about this and had an outline to suggest. He invited us to set it out, and so I outlined what we had in mind, closely tracking the issues I had discussed with Romanow the previous night. In all its essentials, I described a coalition agreement between the Liberals and the NDP modelled on the 1999 Saskatchewan NDP–Liberal coalition. The Liberals agreed to discuss this, point-by-point.

It still seemed to me that things were going too well.

After some fumbling around, we arranged to have a laptop and a projector, so that the text we were working on could be put up on the wall and drafted collectively.

We began with the role of caucuses. We set out our view: the NDP and Liberal caucuses would sit side by side on the government bench. Both would be "government caucuses" with standing to take part in the business of government, but would keep their identities. In other words, we were not proposing to merge our caucuses. Agreed.

Next up: cabinet. We opened by offering a sentence to the effect that nothing in the accord "is intended to diminish or alter the power and prerogatives of the prime minister." We wanted the Liberals to see that we understood modern cabinet government, including the critical role of central agencies led by the prime minister, and were committed to a coherent and effective government. Agreed.

We offered that the prime minister would be the leader of the Liberal Party of Canada—individual unspecified. This was intended to put on paper that it was up to the Liberal caucus who the PM was. Agreed.

Given the panic on the CBC that we might have the effrontery to have our party's long-standing commitment to fiscal responsibility enshrined through an "NDP finance minister," we decided to send a reassuring message to the contrary. So we proposed the agreement detail that the finance minister would also be chosen from the Liberal caucus. Agreed (with relief).

We picked up on Metcalfe's proposal from the previous day and proposed that the accord set out a cabinet of twenty-four ministers. We liked this idea for a number of reasons, the key one being that such a cabinet was small enough to actually meet and discuss issues. That meant cabinet might creep towards becoming a real forum for decision-making after its long sleep. This would be to our benefit as junior partners who did not control the central agencies. Agreed.

We proposed that the cabinet be in the same proportions as our caucuses. The Liberals would be contributing 77 MPs to the government. We would be contributing 37. So we proposed that 8 of the 24 ministers be named from our caucus.

Metcalfe seemed to steel himself. I wrote down what he said next in my notes:

"Some players are questioning the number of cabinet seats," he said. "Some are proposing an accord instead of NDP seats in the cabinet—or an election, instead of doing this agreement."

Katie Telford, Dion's deputy chief of staff, weighed in. She said that the idea of NDP cabinet ministers was just not selling in the Liberal caucus and that it would be more productive for us to work on a different model. The Liberals, she announced, were now prepared to negotiate an accord with us, not a coalition.

So the anvil had dropped. Mr. Dion's team was reneging on the key element of the agreement we had reached the previous day, the core concept that we were forming a coalition government with a joint cabinet.

Dawn Black and I pondered this in silence for some time. Meanwhile, Metcalfe outlined a complex idea that had Jack Layton perhaps sitting in on a Liberal cabinet as some sort of observer without portfolio, perhaps with some role in cabinet committees.

I began by letting a wave of wonderfully intense anger and outrage course through me. I briefly considered aiming some very hot words at the Liberal negotiators.

But I didn't.

I had sat through too many tantrums, too much gross rudeness and incivility across the table during collective bargaining in the film and television industry. In that room on that day we were playing for the highest stakes. It was not the time to import the infantilism I occasionally encountered in my work life.

Anger was followed by a moment of despair. We had been baited and switched. The Liberals had cranked up a national media drama. Our leader had committed a significant share of his political capital into a coalition proposal, which they had agreed to the previous day, but had now taken off the table. They were now offering instead a Peterson–Rae-style accord that we had told them very clearly we were not interested in.

My despair passed quickly. This wasn't a plan. Dion's team didn't look like people who played that way. They were trying this on us because Dion was getting worried about his caucus, and wanted to see if we would agree to an easier sell.

I turned to thinking about how to crack this Liberal position. At the end of the day, I reasoned, Mr. Dion and his team needed an agreement with us more than we needed one with them. If the accord failed, it might damage the NDP to some extent, but our base would see it for what it was, a good try to rid the country of the Conservative government and to replace it with a more progressive one. Mr. Dion on the other hand would not be prime minister and would not be leader of the Liberal Party. It was all-or-nothing for him and his colleagues. So there was no reason to play this game with Mr. Dion's team. It seemed to me what we needed to do was try to get Mr. Dion's negotiators to set out whatever their real bottom line was in this discussion, and then report, so that Jack Layton could take up the matter directly with Mr. Dion.

Dawn Black and I consulted in whispers for a moment. She saw things the same way.

I addressed myself to Metcalfe.

"We don't have a mandate to negotiate an accord with you," I told him. "Would you like us to leave?"

"No," he said.

At which point Marlene Jennings exploded. "I want to say a few things," she said.

She informed us, emphatically, that the coalition proposal was not selling well with her Liberal colleagues because it implied that NDP MPs might gain access to cabinet jobs. Liberal MPs had been waiting for many years for those positions, she explained, and they did not accept that people from some other party might take their places in line.

Dawn Black responded for our side. Over the next half hour or so, Ms. Black ripped Ms. Jennings's argument apart in a fine display of forensic, parliamentarian debate. Two parties would be coming together to form this government, Black explained. All of the members involved had worked very hard during their careers. The new government would only be possible because both parties were involved. Shouldn't simple fairness, and a desire to ensure both parties were equally committed to the success of the government, suggest that both should be represented fairly in the cabinet?

Ms. Jennings defended the entitlements of her caucus colleagues.

Only Liberal MPs, she tried to get us to understand, were qualified for and entitled to cabinet positions.

Ms. Black explained, several times, that this meant there would not be a new government and therefore none of them would be reaching their career goals.

Ms. Jennings then began a rearguard action. She proposed that the NDP could perhaps be accorded a single seat at the cabinet, without a department, in order to monitor what was going on and to make suggestions.

Ms. Black was unmoved by this proposal.

Ms. Jennings offered two seats.

No better luck.

How about three?

Herb Metcalfe, a soft-spoken man, now raised his voice loudly enough that even his own MP heard him. "Maybe we should take a *break,*" he suggested.

While the Liberals regrouped outside the room, Black and I reported back. I BlackBerried Layton and McGrath (1:50 p.m.): "They are getting cold feet on any NDP ministers and are floating an accord. . . . Don't do anything—but be ready that we will jointly ask you to speak directly to Dion to resolve."

McGrath did some checking. She wrote back (1:52 p.m.): "Bloc negotiator says that the Libs have only spoken Lib/NDP coalition and they believe we have to be in." That was a useful lever. The Liberals would find themselves isolated among the Opposition parties unless they returned to the coalition model.

McGrath added (1:59 p.m.): "Ed says Chrétien in favour of cabinet posts too." I replied (2:19 p.m.): "Chrétien should call Dion."

The Liberals returned. Metcalfe noted that the Liberals had just made a significant move, but that the NDP hadn't budged from our opening position. It was our turn to show some flexibility. The Liberals then outlined a proposal they hoped we would consider as an alternative to a significant role in a joint cabinet. Perhaps, in lieu of a proportionate share of seats at the cabinet table, we might accept a third of the parliamentary secretaryships. These parliamentary secretaries would not be just assistants in the House of Commons. They would be sworn in as Privy Councillors with the right to review cabinet documents and to attend meetings when appropriate.

Metcalfe and Jennings went on at some length about how critically important these positions were; how much access they provided; and about why this might be a great way to get New Democrats involved in government without (to translate what they were saying into how we were hearing it) sullying the cabinet table with our presence.

We agreed that one-third of the new government's parliamentary secretaries would be New Democrats. But now we still had to agree to the number of ministers.

Black and I consulted briefly. Clearly we were going to have to make some sort of a move to get this agreement.

We tried the following: I proposed to Metcalfe that the NDP receive seven cabinet positions in a twenty-four-member cabinet. One "major" portfolio (for example, foreign affairs, or a major economic or social portfolio other than finance; perhaps health); three "mid" positions (for example, environment, immigration); and three "small" portfolios (something in the style of the many secretary of state positions with which Prime Minister Harper and many of his predecessors have larded cabinet).

This wasn't much of a move on its face, but to an alert bargainer it was a big signal. We had moved off our principle that the cabinet should be proportionate to the caucuses. We had dropped our "ask" by 12.5 per cent. And we hadn't said any closing words—such as "final and best offer"—so there was still room in our minds for further negotiations.

It didn't seem to us that these signals were picked up by the Liberal team, who still appeared to be having a hard time with the idea of socialists around the big table in any kind of role. Dawn Black and I didn't think we had a mandate to go much farther, especially when it seemed clear the Liberal team didn't have instructions that would get them close enough to us to permit an agreement. It was therefore time to move this discussion to a better level, preferably between Layton and Dion directly, followed by a clean-up session with fewer people involved. Punting the issue out of the room for a while would also have the virtue of creating a window for the Bloc to speak to the Liberals about their unwillingness to support a Liberal-only cabinet.

Black and I therefore suggested a three-step way forward: that we finish the rest of the coalition accord at this session; that we then go back to our principals for further instructions on the issue of the proportions within the cabinet, and perhaps have them speak directly to each other; and that Metcalfe and I then meet one-on-one early the following morning to finalize the government accord.

Agreed.

We went back to the laptop and projector and worked amicably on the rest of the coalition accord.

We agreed on a "no surprises" clause, cribbed from the New Zealand governing accord.

We agreed that "both parties are committed to restoring the integrity, transparency, and efficiency of the appointments process in the public service and in federal bodies like the Supreme Court, the Senate, and commissions like the CRTC. The prime minister will consult the leader of the NDP as appropriate on appointments."

This was a somewhat loaded article. Its implication was that integrity, transparency, and efficiency had been (shall we say) issues in the past. The Liberals were likely thinking about recent Tory appointments. We had in mind the way the Liberals had conducted themselves in office in the slightly-less-recent past. These words gave us grounds to challenge questionable appointments, and an expectation of being consulted. It was about as deep an encroachment into the prime minister's currently untrammelled power of appointment as we could reasonably seek without overreaching. The Liberals added the word "efficiency" to this paragraph to seed the idea that the Conservatives had gone too far in some of their anti-corruption legislation, making it impossible for the federal government to recruit many possibly desirable candidates.

The Liberals proposed, and we agreed to, a "standing committee of the accord," chaired by the prime minister. They had drawn this idea from some of their own reading of other coalition accords. It created a formal mechanism for coalition principals to meet regularly to make sure the coalition was on track. We stapled into this the idea of a committee of respected party leaders who would assist in dealing with disputes. Agreed. And we were done.

We adjourned to report to our principals. We had a completed coalition accord, with one issue outstanding. We wanted seven cabinet seats out of twenty-four. The last Liberal offer was three.

We returned and reported in detail to Layton, Blakeney, Broadbent, and McGrath about how the negotiations had gone, what we had achieved so far, and the remaining sticking point.

The issue of our deputation in the cabinet was a tricky one. In principle, we wanted enough of a team to have at least one minister from every region of the country. One from BC, one from the Prairies, one from Toronto (Layton), one from either Northern or industrial Ontario; one from Quebec; one from the Atlantic. It was hard to get smaller than that, and that gave us a fairly hard bottom line of six seats.

On the other hand, we had to consider the equally tricky issue of how Layton could simultaneously be a cabinet minister and fulfill his duties as the NDP federal leader. He could handle the work (as many European party leaders do). The issue was whether or not he would have the resources to do the job. Presumably, in the six-seat scenario, he would be able to combine his present office plus a minister's office, giving him a fairly good base from which to work, but we thought a better solution might be to have him appointed deputy prime minister, with a less-improvised team. So that became our bottom line on the cabinet issue—five seats, plus a deputy prime ministership for Layton, or six seats so we would have the bones of a national ministerial team.

I summarized what happened next in my notebook:

Layton to Duceppe, Duceppe to Dion—no coalition, no accord. Broadbent to Chrétien, Chrétien to Dion—don't blow this.

Layton and the rest of our team brought Dawn Black and me up to speed on their own discussions about policy. They had had a productive day, working up the details of an economic stimulus and income-security package that we could present to the Liberals on Sunday. A lot of homework had been generated that was going to keep Emily Watkins and the rest of the NDP research team busy late into the night.

In due course I caught up on my e-mails and called around to see what we could learn about what was happening within the red team and what might be coming from the blue team. I jotted down the bits and pieces I hunted and gathered:

Bluegrits—counterrevolution developing on their side. Angry Toronto business liberals. Peter Donolo, et al. Iggy to the big chair. Best if people miss plane [to the key votes to defeat the Tories].

Tory side—Flaherty—lose right to strike. No $. Won't go there. Giornio's gambit—prorogue the house. Tories are signalling their willingness to consider discussions. What are our demands?

Visceral rage at Dion. They hate him. A quote from a party insider passed along to us: "There is no fucking way that asshole who ruined our party will get any benefit from this."

Ferocious anti-Bloc mood. Fight the separatists.

[More gossiping about Senator] Smith—Furious about idea of Dion. Get David to explain stupid socialists . . . Painful experience [working with Dion]. Of all Lib leaders, most painful of his life. Not a happy camper at all.

Tories prorogue argument. "Don't—time out."

[Article by] Scott Reid—First things first. Take him out. Harper gone. Tories fall down. Don't get fancy—put Harper in his grave. [More excellent advice on this theme, which perhaps we should have taken.]

Kathleen Monk reported from her conversations with journalists (8:07 p.m.): "They think Harper will bring the Bloc on board by buying them outright. Flaherty tomorrow will announce a doubling of infrastructure money. They will roll over on the refusal of right to strike and likely on pay equity by Monday. Basically a total fold on behalf of the Cons. They think our chances—once 50-50—are now far less."

Karl Bélanger added, the same minute (8:07 p.m.): "Rumour here is prorogation on Friday. Throne Speech and budget early January."

In between gossip-collecting, I tried to see how Metcalfe was coming along on our remaining issue. I called him for the first time at 7:00 p.m., and left a message on his cell phone. I echoed this with a BlackBerry note telling him I'd left him a message, my phone number attached. At 7:27 p.m. he replied: "Do you have anything from your side?" I replied: "I have a bit of room to manoeuvre." Metcalfe (7:37 p.m.): "I think I can get some movement but would help if I had an idea of what room you have."

Jack Layton and Anne McGrath left Centre Block to attend the annual press gallery dinner.

I called Metcalfe, and this time he picked up my call. We spoke briefly, dancing around each other. Metcalfe told me he had been authorized to canvass the leadership candidates about the issue.

I reported my conversation with Metcalfe to Layton on his BlackBerry (9:05 p.m.): "Heard from Libs. They are canvassing three leadership candidates on Dion proposal to offer four seats. I told them not to make that a bottom line, but they're close. They agreed to leave themselves some flex." Via Layton's BlackBerry, Anne McGrath replied (9:32 p.m.): "Anne here. Showed this message to Jack. He nodded."

Later that night I wrote the following in my notebook:

Metcalfe to Rae—five. Metcalfe to Ignatieff—difficult discussion wants to win through usual route. [Reply to Ignatieff] Road to failure, blow chance. Grudgingly agreed. Wants to be @ table.
Lib associations petitioning MPs to do this.

Around one in the morning, Layton and McGrath returned from the press gallery dinner. They reported seeing Ignatieff and Kory Teneycke, Prime Minister Stephen Harper's communications director, huddled together in an intense conversation that went on for some time.

That didn't sound encouraging.

It was time to call it a day.

Sunday,
November 30, 2008

THE BLACKBERRY FLOOD STARTED EARLY FOR A SUNDAY.

Kathleen Monk (8:18 a.m.): "Iggy will be on *Newsworld* at 9 a.m. Baird will follow. Apparently Iggy and Kory T. were seen having lengthy tête-à-tête last night at the gallery dinner." In the morning light that still didn't sound good.

Dawn Black (8:26 a.m.): "Ujjal. We just spoke. He said we must be hard line—not give an inch to the Conservatives no matter what they bring forward. His view was that Peter J[ulian] and Paul Dewar left an impression on TV we would consider a new package if one is brought forward from the Conservatives." (This, of course, is exactly what Dosanjh and his Liberal colleagues themselves would agree to do only a few days later.)

Herb Metcalfe and I met for breakfast in the restaurant in the Delta Hotel in downtown Ottawa. We loaded up on comfort food for what was going to be a long day, and got down to business.

By 9:09 a.m., the cards were on the table.

I BlackBerried a report to Dawn Black, so that she could brief Jack

Layton and the rest of the team that was meeting at NDP caucus office: "[The Liberals] offered eight parliamentary secretaryships. Agreed that if PM feels he must have more than 24 ministries, our proportion would be maintained. They offered five seats. I countered with five + deputy PM, or six seats. Liberal negotiator is choking on deputy PM because if Liberal PM is run over by a bus, we're PM. I offered to write a line that this won't happen. No take-up. We've recessed. He's off to talk to Dion. Will get back at 9:30 or so. I think he'll recommend six seats in a 25+1 cabinet (i.e., another Lib added too). He believes scenario is Dion will be PM until May, and then be replaced by a new leader, likely Ignatieff. We gossiped. Rae easy. Ignatieff extremely reluctant. Dion listening to Chrétien, who was very tough with them last night."

While Herb Metcalfe was off consulting his leader and his fractious tribe, I sat at our restaurant table catching up on my e-mail tsunami and doodling in my notebook. I tried to summarize the risks and rewards of what we were doing.

I started with the short-term risks we faced:

Tories buy Ignatieff and blue Libs with a stimulus package.
Tories prorogue to January.
NDP caucus bucks deal.
Tory communications plan works.

As it turned out, all of these risks came true except for the risk that our caucus would refuse to back a coalition agreement.

Trying to be more positive, I summarized the benefits we might hope for.

If we succeed:
Role in ministry.
Federal party stops being poor cousin.
Sets up next campaign—candidates, organizers, etc. $ will improve.
Will have a record to run on.

I liked the idea that the federal NDP would have a direct role in the government for many reasons, a key one being that it would change the federal NDP, by giving it direct exposure to the realities of government. One of the realities of the New Democratic Party is that electorally successful sections—our Western Canadian sections—occasionally must struggle against the temptation to patronize developing sections who have yet to win. The federal party has been the beneficiary of priceless support from provincial sections with experience in government. But being at the centre of the federal government would transform the relationship in a healthy way, I thought.

I mused that succeeding in this enterprise might set up our next campaign nicely, by which I meant a better-funded air-and-ground campaign (a $35- to $40-million proposition) aiming for victory in 160+ ridings in a succeeding general election. I had been campaign director the two previous campaigns. Campaign directors think in terms of candidates, message, organization, and money.

Finally, I liked the idea of having a record to run on. The NDP budget had served us well. It would be helpful to have something new to campaign on next time.

I went back to the downsides:

If we fail:
Ignatieff and blue Liberals will have killed it.
Need to keep government and policy asks modest so can't be accused of overreaching in negotiations.
Make Ignatieff wear Harper government for rest of his career.
Split Lib caucus? Break NGOs and Lib-labour to us for failure to take opportunity.
Risk: NDP too hot for government. 'Responsible.' Tory concessions take sting out.

Here again, alas, much of what worried me that morning came to pass and little of what we hoped for did in the short term.

Metcalfe was gone somewhat longer than expected. Eventually, he returned looking a little flustered. The police had pulled him over and he had received an ill-timed traffic ticket. This BlackBerry exchange with Jack Layton tells the tale of what happened next:

Me to Jack Layton (10:13 a.m.): "Final offer: They are offering 5 ministers + 8 parliamentary secretaryships/privy councillors. No to DPM. No to 6. 24 ministers + PM. If a larger cabinet is selected, then our proportions are maintained. Instructions please."

We marked time while our principals talked directly to each other. Ed Broadbent and Jean Chrétien discussed this issue and agreed on six. Then they spoke to their principals with this advice. Eventually, Metcalfe looked at his buzzing BlackBerry and then looked at me.

"Okay, it's six," he said.

We shook hands and the government accord was complete.

Me to Layton (10:58 a.m.): "Excellent work well done. Everything signed and sealed."

Whew!

Back in the boardroom of NDP caucus office, Layton, Broadbent and Blakeney were meeting with a fairly large group of NDP research and communications staffers. When I joined them with the government accord in hand, they focused intensely on our policy proposals. The room was close and hot, and the federal NDP staff seemed a little shell-shocked from the morning they had spent with Layton and our two party saints. It is a formidable thing to be cross-examined by either Allan Blakeney or Ed Broadbent. To get this simultaneously, in stereo, plus the attentions of the federal leader was probably a pretty good character-building exercise for our team.

I had agreed to a work plan with Metcalfe after we finished the government accord. We planned to resume our discussions with a Liberal–NDP bilateral meeting on the policy accord beginning at noon. We would then jointly present our accord to the Bloc Québécois at 3:00 p.m. and ask them for their support in the house.

That left me about forty-five minutes to get familiar with the policy work our team had been working on line by line for the better part of two days—an impossible job. So I waited for a brief silence in the discussion and then inserted myself to talk about what we were going to do next.

We were due back to Salon D on the second floor of the Sheraton at 12:30 p.m. and we needed to finalize who our delegation would be. I proposed myself, Blakeney, Broadbent, Black, and McGrath. Agreed.

I then proposed, for several reasons, that Blakeney and Broadbent take turns presenting our policy proposals to the Liberals. First, they had just spent many hours squeezing each word of those proposals, and so knew exactly what Jack Layton and the rest of our team were looking for. Second, they were highly credible spokespeople on public-policy issues and were more immune than most of us to charges of recklessness and irresponsibility. Assuming we succeeded, we would be looking to Blakeney and Broadbent to help Layton explain what we were trying to achieve, both to our internal audiences (the caucus, the party, the labour movement, and the broader progressive left in Canada) and to external ones (our voters and those we hoped would become our voters). They therefore needed to have the policy issues in their DNA, and there is no better way to master a brief than to have to present it in a negotiation. Agreed.

Our staff quickly finalized our pitch document. We grabbed a quick bite to eat, and then we gathered ourselves together and set off to the hotel two blocks away for the next round of talks with our new friends and allies on the red team.

We settled back into the tight, non-descript meeting room at the Sheraton. The Liberal delegation was again led by Metcalfe, joined by Ralph Goodale and Marlene Jennings and a rotating cast of Liberal staff members, including, most of the time, Dion chief of staff Sénécal and deputy chief of staff Telford. The tone was friendly and businesslike. With the governing accord under our belts we knew we were in sight of an agreement, provided we could come to terms on our basic agenda.

We discussed how to proceed, agreeing that the NDP would start off by setting out our proposals. We would then adjourn, the Liberals would consider their counter-proposal, and then we'd see if we had enough overlap to find an agreement.

Volunteers and staff on both sides of the table now stepped back. It was time for our party's statesmen and stateswomen to carry the negotiations.

Blakeney and Broadbent began by reiterating the basic understanding we had arrived at on Friday. The new government's job was to address the present economic crisis, and all of its focus would be on economic issues. Speaking for the Liberals, Goodale agreed.

Our team then presented our proposals verbally and in writing. We wanted four things.

First, we wanted the policy accord to spell out the New Democratic Party's commitment to fiscal responsibility, a commitment we knew Goodale was also passionate about. Blakeney had been one of Roy Romanow's closest counsellors when Romanow struggled to save Saskatchewan from bankruptcy in the early 1990s, courtesy of another reckless tax-cutting Conservative government. Some of Blakeney's proudest achievements as premier, including what remained of the province's dental and drug plans, had been lost while our government dealt with $15 billion of public debt sitting on fewer than 300,000 taxpayers.

Ralph Goodale also knew what Conservative fiscal recklessness had done to his home province, and shared our views on this matter. We wanted it hardwired into the governing accord. That meant a commitment that the budget would be rebalanced once the economic crisis was mastered.

Second, we wanted the new government to commit to a strong economic stimulus package, focused on infrastructure investments. Jack Layton paid particularly close attention to this part of our package during our discussions. As a former Toronto city councillor and president of the Federation of Canadian Municipalities, Layton had a detailed understanding of the gaping infrastructure deficits blighting our economy in every part of the country. He also knew how quickly municipal authorities could get to work on new projects if funded, and he knew what a major difference investment in this area could make to people's lives. We wanted to see a strong commitment to new infrastructure, to housing and housing retrofit, and to a renewal of Canada's manufacturing and resource industries.

Third, we wanted families that had been hurt in the recession to get some help, immediately. In three previous federal campaigns, we had told the people of Canada we would fight in Parliament for working families. Journalists made gagging sounds when we said this. But we meant it. The top-of-mind issue for many policy-makers in the Western world, as they work through the consequences of small "c" conservative misrule, is what to do to repair the balance sheets of banks and major corporations. Our top-of-mind issue was what to do for the working families who are paying and will continue to pay a double price for the incompetence of their betters: the loss of their livelihoods, while they are expected to bail out their bosses with their taxes. We wanted measures to help the rising tide of unemployed meet their mortgages, pay their bills, and be given some hope for future employment. We had three measures in mind: enhanced training; restoring Employment Insurance; and expanding the child benefit, an excellent vehicle for redistributing wealth to low-income working families hardest hit in the recession.

Finally, the policy accord needed an "and another thing" section to deal with some specific issues. The Tories had lost their majority in Quebec in part because of foolish insensitivity about issues affecting cultural industries. We wanted attention paid to that. Allan Blakeney did one for the home team by putting the Canadian Wheat Board and supply management on the agenda. And we wanted to see our environmental agenda woven into the accord—nicely packaged into a continentalist vision, so that our Liberal coalition partners could accept it.

This was all presented. Goodale asked some clarification questions and offered some preliminary comments. Then we adjourned, heading down the hall to wait in another bleak boardroom while the Liberal team settled down to consider their response.

I caught up on e-mails. Dawn Black had an interesting report from a Liberal contact (12:56 p.m.): "I just heard from a friend of Michael. He was only able to speak to his press liaison at this point. He said our read on it is correct. The Libs need to iron out how long Dion stays, what he stays to do. What is less defined—in time as it is in milestones—i.e., budget. They don't seem to know where the line will be drawn between Dion and his successor."

That was interesting. A potential compromise between Dion and Ignatieff, in which Dion could serve as prime minister for a time, but then agree to cede his place to either Ignatieff or Rae after their spring convention.

I reported to Layton on how things were going. He quizzed me closely on a key detail of our proposal: that 1 per cent of the GST be transferred to municipal governments to fund infrastructure and operations.

I wrote (1:48 p.m.): "Goodale opposes transferring federal tax points and argued for quantifying the amount, i.e. $7 billion not 1 per cent of GST."

Layton (1:50 p.m.): "I can agree. Is he talking three years? It can be noted in communications that is equivalent to 1 per cent of GST. That is the exact language of the FCM position—I negotiated the introduction of the word 'equivalent' with David Miller. We'll back channel with calls to the mayors from me to ensure they come hard on board."

Me (1:54 p.m.): "No deal yet. They adjourned and are formulating a response. Just reporting his musings."

Layton (1:59 p.m.): "Got it. What's your sense of the tone and reaction of their team?"

Me (2:03 p.m.): "These are the people who dismantled the federal government in the 1990s. I think they're going to try to avoid specific commitments."

It was now time for the skilful folks in the Prime Minister's Office to try to drop a bomb in the middle of our negotiations.

The raw material they had to work with was a transcript of an NDP caucus meeting teleconference held the previous day, apparently taped by Vancouver Conservative MP John Duncan, an inadvertent invitee due to a name mix-up by a junior NDP staff member.

The Prime Minister's Office leaked this transcript to *CTV News*, which promptly aired it. A key focus of the network's reporting was a snippet from Layton's leader's report to caucus, in which he reviewed the discussions he had had with the Bloc through the FTQ earlier that fall, exploring the possibility of replacing the Conservatives.

This was not news to the NDP caucus, but it caused some impressive hyperventilating on air. The NDP had been *plotting* with the *separatists*.

Anne McGrath reported the effect of this news on our negotiations in an admirably understated e-mail to Layton (2:51 p.m.): "Brian and Dawn have been in sidebar discussions to calm down the Liberal team," she reported to Layton. "This is definitely not helpful. I think we should not have any more conference calls."

Indeed.

However, once the shouting had stopped and it came down to brass tacks with Herb Metcalfe, the Liberals shrugged the leak off and we got back to work.

At about 3:00 p.m., we returned to the main boardroom to hear the Liberal counter-proposal. They had been drafting with a laptop and projector, and walked us through their counter-proposal line-by-line. Blakeney, Broadbent, and Black asked detailed questions, paragraph by paragraph. Essentially, all of our proposals were reflected in their version, in much less detail and with no spending commitments attached. There was one key omission: they did not want to include any reference to an enhanced child benefit or to child care.

It was time for another Dawn Black moment.

Black picked up the cudgel, demanding to know what the Liberals had against families and children, especially given all the complaining they had done about the fate of their last-days-of-Martin press releases about child care.

The Liberal front line seemed extremely embarrassed to have to defend the position they were taking, and, as the discussion proceeded, more and more of the Liberal talking was being done by their leader's office research staffer.

He argued, relentlessly and repetitively, that no spending commitments must be made that would be "structural spending." Helping families and children, to his mind, was "structural spending," and so nothing could be done about child poverty or the real-world consequences of unemployment to average Canadian families.

It was fascinating to watch the Liberal team during this exchange. They looked ashamed of themselves. They also looked defeated and powerless. How many times during their recent decade in office, I wondered, had elected Liberals worn expressions like that on their faces, while staff and bureaucrats chanted neo-con blather? Permanent tax cuts for wealthy individuals and business were "investments." Help for poor families was "structural spending."

Black was on a bottom line. She spelled it out for the arrogant young Liberal staffer. If there was nothing about child poverty and child care in the agreement, Black said, then there would be no agreement and no coalition government.

Ed Broadbent, author of a landmark motion in the House of Commons calling for concrete steps to end child poverty in Canada, which was unanimously adopted, backed her up strongly.

Blakeney caught Goodale's eye. What if we put in a very clear commitment on this issue, with the note that we will move forward "as finances permit"? Goodale jumped at this solution, and into the accord it went: "As finances permit, we are committed to move forward with improved child benefits and an early learning and childcare program in partnership with each province, and respectful of their role and jurisdiction, including the possibility of opt out with full compensation."

Agreed.

It was time to check with headquarters, and to decide if we had what we needed.

In essence, the Liberals were doing to us what they do to the Canadian public every election. They had picked up on our themes and priorities, stripped out the operating detail, and had fed the resulting comforting words back to us to persuade us that a progressive agenda would be pursued, while avoiding any detailed or concrete commitments.

Should we play along with this?

Each member of our negotiating team had to make up his or her own mind about that. I was inclined to work with what was before us, for several reasons.

First, I was mindful that no plan survives contact with the enemy, especially in the context of a major economic crisis. Our team had worked hard on our proposals. But could we really be sure we had anticipated every contingency that might occur to Canada's national government over the next two years? Likely not.

Second, I knew that an overly detailed policy agenda can be a trap.

In provincial politics, policy specifics are sometimes helpful. You commit to pave fifty kilometres of that road. At some point during your four-year term, you do it. Next election you point to the road, and promise with credibility to do the next stretch.

On the other hand, policy specifics that seemed smart at the time do not always turn out to be so. A few years ago I attended a retirement party for a colleague in the government of Saskatchewan. I was seated next to our then-newly-appointed justice minister, whose first words in his life to me were: "So you're the stupid ass who promised to hire three hundred more police officers." There had indeed been such a commitment in our 1999 election platform that I might have had something to do with. We were trying to communicate our commitment to safe communities. Perhaps it was good politics at the time (it had worked for Bill Clinton), but it would seem that this specific proposal had proved challenging to implement, given the many other pressures in the justice and corrections system.

Third, there was the rhythm of the negotiation to consider. Our counterparty had invested heavily in an internal debate late into the previous night to meet us on a position from which we would not budge—we intended to be in the ministry if we were to support a new government. Insisting on the letter and form of our policy draft might force them into a similar process again. Would they come around to our point of view a second time? Or would they conclude they were dealing with an overly greedy partner and refuse to close? Likely the latter. When you are a cat and you already have a pretty good canary in your mouth, it is time to think about how the other side gets one too, so that you get to keep your canary. This being so, it was better in my view to let the Liberals author a key coalition document, and therefore have cause to hope they would be able to shape and lead a government in which they would have 66 per cent of the caucus and 75 per cent of the ministry.

Finally, the Liberal policy draft was at least putting most of the right issues on the agenda. Unlike (apparently) Liberal ministers and backbenchers, we wouldn't be powerless in the face of obdurate and regressive positions from neo-con staffers in the proposed government's leader's office. Our team would retain their identity and leverage as a separate party, and would be in a position to insist on progress on those files, whether or not the price tags and operating details were included in the coalition policy accord.

I wrote to Layton (3:37 p.m.): "They are proposing we be silent on price tags on commitments . . . in return for basically accepting our entire list. Is that ok?" Layton took some time to think about it, and then replied with admirable brevity (4:05 p.m.): "Yes."

We caucused. The rest of our bargaining team were of like mind in the circumstances. We would work with the Liberal draft, as amended.

So, we told the Liberals we had a deal.

Next up, the Bloc.

The Liberals had been meeting with the Bloc and seemed to feel confident that no fundamental issues stood in the way of securing their agreement to support the new government. We tested this through our own channel to the Bloc team, who reported back shortly before the Bloc team arrived at the hotel for their own discussions with the now-united Liberal–NDP team. Karl Bélanger (3:38 p.m.): "The Bloc will bring the language issue to the table and would like our support."

I knew what that meant.

For some months, the Bloc Québécois had been agitating in the house on language issues, the topic Quebec ethnic nationalists go to when they feel their agenda is boring voters. The angle the Bloc was working turned on the applicability of the Quebec language charter to federally regulated companies—specifically banks, telephone companies, and certain transportation companies. The Bloc wanted the federal Parliament to legislate that all federally regulated companies must respect Quebec's language laws. As they knew, our party supported this position on the argument that French-speaking workers should have the right to work in their own language in Quebec.

Bélanger was giving us the heads-up that the Bloc wanted to see this issue addressed in the policy accord.

We marked time while the Liberal office meticulously proofread and translated the government and policy accords we had negotiated during the preceding forty-eight hours.

Finally, at about 6:00 p.m., the Bloc negotiating team arrived in our little boardroom. Their team was headed by Gilles Duceppe's chief of staff, François Leblanc. They greeted the Liberals frostily and us fairly warmly. Leblanc pulled me aside to tell me what they were going to do.

"Look, we're separatists and fighting for separatism is mostly what we're about," he began.

A great start to a beautiful relationship, I thought.

But since that issue was not going to be on the front burner for a few years, he continued, they were ready to focus on having a better government in office in Ottawa. What they intended to do was try to get a win for French-speaking Quebecers in the coalition accord. To that end, they were going to raise the language issue and make the following offer: if the government undertook to address it in some fashion, the Bloc would commit to support the new government in Parliament until June 2011—two-and-a-half years. If the coalition did not agree to make this commitment, then the Bloc would take a year off the table, and agree to support the new government only until June 2010.

I had my instructions on this matter. I told Leblanc we supported the right to work in French in Quebec in both provincial and federal jurisdictions. I also told him I didn't know where the Liberals stood on this issue.

We all sat down, the Liberals and Bloc across from each other, and the NDP team clustered at the head of the table out of direct line of fire. The Bloc staff had been given drafts of the accords and had numerous quibbles with the quality of the French drafting, as well as some useful detail on some of the policy points. For example, they helpfully proposed to toughen up the language in the accord on environmental policy, specifying that 1990 be the base year for a new cap-and-trade system to control carbon emissions.

We quickly got down to their two key issues. They wanted a clause in the policy accord that clearly spelled out exactly what kind of support they were committing to provide the Liberal–NDP coalition government. And they played their language card, offering us June 2011 with it, or June 2010 without.

What followed was a discursive, sometimes confusing, discussion that flowed back and forth about the two issues.

The discussion about the form of the Bloc's support for the new government in the house was highly technical. They had consulted some parliamentary experts and proposed a complex clause to govern this matter. We spent some time going back and forth trying to understand their intent.

Finally, Allan Blakeney asked for a pause in the discussion, and asked me for a complete translation of the wording on the table and what had been said about it. We took a time out while I attempted a free-form translation of the obscurely worded legalistic French text projected on the wall and provided a summary of the discussion to date. Blakeney, Broadbent, and Black discussed it for a while, and then Blakeney set out what we needed to do. The text proposed by the Bloc was too complex and vague for the new government to rely on. We needed an unambiguous commitment from the Bloc that it would support the new government on all supply and confidence votes in the house. Blakeney repeated this to the table once we reassembled. He proposed that the Liberals and NDP discuss the issue between ourselves and that we make a counter-proposal on this issue. Agreed.

The Bloc set out their offer on the language issue: more time for the government, in return for a commitment to address the language issue in some appropriate manner. Johanne Sénécal discussed this proposal in civil terms with the Bloc negotiators for some time, trying to find a construction of words that the Bloc could live with that did not require the Liberals to make this commitment. The Bloc stuck to their position. Marlene Jennings then spoke up. Glaring at the Bloc negotiators, she told them emphatically that the Liberal Party would never accept any such proposal and that it was absolutely, flatly, completely, and for all time out of the question (she would later boast about this intervention in a local newspaper in her riding, saying that she had forced the Bloc to abandon "separatism" during the term of the proposed agreement, a victory that would perhaps have been news to Mr. Leblanc).

The Bloc negotiators didn't respond well to the tone of this intervention, and were clearly gearing up for a shouting match. This being so, I spoke up, and proposed that we deal with this matter the same way Allan Blakeney had suggested we deal with the question of parliamentary support. I asked for time for the Liberals and the NDP to discuss the file, and said we would then make a proposal. With some relief, the Bloc team agreed to this. They said they were going to leave and return to their office, and that, when we were ready, we could call them to give them our "offers." On this charmless note, at about 8:00 p.m., the Bloc permanently left the formal coalition negotiations (although they would continue to work amicably and productively with Sénécal and her team bilaterally and informally until Mr. Harper prorogued the house).

The NDP and Liberal teams ordered up some dinner and turned to considering what we would propose to the Bloc. I spoke privately with Ralph Goodale and Johanne Sénécal to see what could be done about the language issue. Basically, they said this was a non-starter in their caucus for reasons that should be obvious given how the discussion had gone. Goodale said that the Bloc's offer of support until June 2010 was probably quite acceptable. As a practical matter (as the Tories were about to prove to us), the government could manoeuvre in the house to survive long after June 2010. Many things could happen then. The Bloc might support a June 2011 budget on its merits. Or perhaps we might welcome them voting to defeat a June 2011 budget, to provide a helpful frame for a new election.

I reported this to our delegation.

If I can indulge in another laugh-out-loud understatement, it would be fair to say that the Western Canadian members of our team were not keen to put our party in the middle of another debate about language laws. We phoned home and asked our mother ship for instructions. We concluded that this was an issue we could work on within government. We should not let it keep Mr. Harper in office. We therefore agreed to go along with the Liberals' proposal that the coalition government accept the Bloc's offer of support until June 2010.

Then we turned to the question of the form of a parliamentary commitment from the Bloc.

Blakeney repeated our basic goal. We wanted them to undertake to support the government on all supply and confidence motions until at least June 2010. We took a look at the 1985 Peterson–Rae accord, which contained some useful language governing this matter. Goodale then got on the phone with his parliamentary expert, and we worked to craft the appropriate paragraphs, setting out in plain language that the government would not seek its own defeat, and the Bloc would not vote to defeat it during the term of the agreement. In due course, we had the words we needed.

The Liberal staff gathered up the drafts. They undertook to communicate our proposals to the Bloc, which the Bloc would grumpily accept later that night, subject to editing. The Liberal team also said they would see to the translation and finalization of all the documents, and would think through the details of how all of this would be announced to the people of Canada the following day. We would be informed once they had made those decisions.

Being in control of the paperwork and the process seemed to be extremely important to the Liberal team.

We then broke up, with little drama, and handshakes all around.

On our part, the NDP team was eager for some sleep. On their part, the unfortunate Liberal staffers knew they were in for a very long night of translating, drafting, and discussion with their boss and their various stakeholders.

It was about 11:00 p.m. Sunday night. We had the deal. Some of our delegation went home to bed. A few of us gathered in Jack Layton's office to report to him and the rest of his senior team, and then to mark the occasion with a modest but fitting glass of scotch.

We knew we had two jobs to do the following day. In the morning, we needed to present the agreement to the NDP caucus and to secure their support. And in the afternoon we needed to join the Liberals and the Bloc to present the agreement to the people of Canada.

Monday,
December 1, 2008

THE NDP CAUCUS MET AT 9:00 A.M.

Many things about our political system are currently invisible to citizens. What lies above the water on the evening news is made up of increasingly brief snippets from party leaders. The result is that Canadian politics looks like a gladiatorial fight between a sitting president and two or three rivals hoping to replace him. But as the fate of Stéphane Dion just a few days later would demonstrate, a great deal more goes on in Parliament than exchanges of talking points between leaders. Of immediate moment, nothing really important happens in a political party without the ultimate support of its caucus of MPs.

Our task on Monday morning was therefore to brief the NDP caucus on our work over the weekend, and then to offer them a plausible case for why they should proceed with the agreements. This had never been accomplished before. Off and on over the previous fifty years, opportunities to build formal partnerships with other parties in minority Parliaments had come and gone. The farmer–labour, CCF, and NDP caucuses had always rejected such initiatives.

Layton asked Blakeney, Broadbent, Black, and I to present the coalition agreements and to argue for them. We sat together in a row on one side of a pleasingly large caucus table, comparing notes on how we would divide up the presentation (I had seen much smaller NDP caucus meetings after previous elections). For good or ill, I had led our negotiations. I would kick off. Blakeney would walk the caucus through the details of the agreements. Broadbent would make the political case for going into coalition. Black would wrap up our presentation and make the closing pitch.

Many of our newly-elected MPs were from Ontario and, like me, had joined the party when Ed Broadbent was leader. They had not had the privilege of serving with him in caucus, so a half-dozen lined up to shake Broadbent's hand and tell him how much they admired his contribution to the cause. Since they knew why he was there, this seemed to me to be a hopeful sign of what mood our Members of Parliament were in.

The meeting began. Layton framed the discussion and then called on us to present our report.

I opened by thanking my colleagues and shared how privileged I felt to work with them on such an interesting file. I drew the caucus's attention to the draft agreements, and outlined them in summary, knowing that Blakeney would follow with a line-by-line analysis.

I didn't know how I was going to wrap up my report. The room was absolutely, unnervingly silent and motionless.

Decorating the walls were posters and photos of all of the party's former leaders: Woodsworth, who had fought in the early days of the farmer-labour ginger group and had been the CCF's first leader; Coldwell; Douglas; Lewis; Broadbent (sitting in the flesh to my right). McLaughlin; McDonough. I felt all their eyes on me. I decided to talk to them and their caucuses as well as to the present one.

Why, I asked, had so many poor people and so many workers contributed precious dimes and quarters to send farmer-labour, CCF, and NDP MPs to Ottawa for all these years? Their tiny contributions were a very big thing to them—for many, they represented a decision about what their families would eat that week. Did they do that so that we could come to Ottawa and issue press releases? They did that so MPs representing them could kick the wealthy and privileged out of office, take over the state, and put it to work for ordinary working people. That meant reaching for political power when it was there to be had, and using it to get as much done as possible in the practical circumstances of the time. That meant accepting responsibility for the consequences of using that power. That meant getting real results, not just talking about doing so.

I went on in this vein for a few more minutes—to the point when I could feel Blakeney shifting ever so subtly in his seat, getting across the message: "You are starting to go over the top." Time to shut up. I did.

This intervention seemed to be well-received.

Blakeney was next. He put on his glasses and called our caucus's attention to the documents. In much cooler tones than I had hit, he went line-by-line through the government and policy accords, pointing out the implications of the agreements, their internal compromises and silences, the policy risks we were running, and rewards we might hope for. He recommended that caucus accept the accords.

Broadbent turned to the issue of whether or not it was sensible to go into coalition with the Liberal Party of Canada. He reviewed the history of the Peterson–Rae accord, of his own dealings with Pierre Trudeau after the 1980 election, and the risks and potential rewards of this current proposal. He argued that, if we had the balance of power, we should use it. Unlike the situation in 1980, the last time an NDP–Liberal coalition was seriously considered, we were in that position now. Further, he noted, "it was critical to have NDP ministers to be seen to be doing things, and not just talking." He recommended caucus accept the accords.

Dawn Black wrapped up our presentation. She picked up on the theme of why people sent us to Ottawa, but zeroed in on her own constituents, what they hoped for and needed. She talked about the joys and frustrations of being an Opposition MP, and predicted that being on the government side would be even more difficult. She argued it would be worth it, and so she recommended caucus adopt the accords.

It was now time for the MPs to have their say. Most spoke, working within the brutal time limits that permit a thirty-seven-member deliberative body to talk to itself.

Jack Layton wrapped up. This was an opportunity to get some real change in Canada, he argued. It was an opportunity to keep our commitments to the people of Canada to use whatever political power they gave us in Parliament to get real results. He urged acceptance, and put the accords to a vote.

They were approved.

While our caucus was deliberating, my BlackBerry had been buzzing with a steady stream of e-mails back and forth between us and the Liberals and the Bloc, mostly about editing details and announcement logistics. François Leblanc from the Bloc and Johanne Sénécal from Dion's office had begun e-mailing each other at 7:19 a.m. that morning, with copies to us.

At 8:27 a.m., Sénécal set out how she saw that day unfolding: *"Je suis en voiture et serais au bureau dans 15 min. Je t'appele a 9 heures. Nous avons un caucus à midi. L'idée que j'ai en tête mais doit encore vous en parlez—vous et NPD—serait d'avoir une rencontre à trois en apres-midi pour signer les documents et point de presse."* ["I'm in my car and will be in the office in 15 minutes. I'll call you at 9:00 a.m. We have a caucus at noon. What I'm considering but I need to speak to you about—you and the NDP—is to have a three-sided meeting this afternoon to sign the documents and then a press conference."]

At 11:14 a.m., I wrote to Sénécal: "Our caucus would like to be reassured that these documents are final and that your colleagues won't seek to roll back or fundamentally amend them. Do you suppose I can tell them that we have an agreement in final form on all substantive points?"

She replied (11:24 a.m.): "I cannot get you that. Our caucus has to see it first. But you can report that all three leadership candidates are very comfortable with the agreement." I replied (11:32 a.m.): "Ok. Hopefully the leadership candidates will get listened to."

I checked the news on my BlackBerry. Ignatieff, Rae, and Leblanc had met in Ignatieff's condo the previous night. They would be holding a joint press conference to announce they were fully supportive of the coalition and of their leader.

Our caucus ended. I joined Layton's team in his office, and we kept an eye on CBC *Newsworld* as the Liberal caucus met. They approved the accords. Dion announced he would remain as Liberal leader for the time being, but would step down in favour of a successor to be elected at the Liberal convention in May.

Sénécal wrote to Leblanc and me at 2:01 p.m.: "Let's meet at 2:15 once QP starts to talk about next steps. *Prochaines étapes: signature des documents et conference de presse conjointe* [Next steps: signature of documents and joint press conference]."

CTV Ottawa Bureau Chief Robert Fife had another scoop. He reported that the Liberals and the NDP had agreed to create a four-person economic panel to guide the new government on finance, budget, and economic issues. This committee would be made up of the four most credible leaders from the two parties on these issues: former prime minister Paul Martin, former New Brunswick premier Frank McKenna, former deputy prime minister John Manley, and former Saskatchewan premier Roy Romanow.

It sounded like a pretty good idea to me.

The only thing surprising about it was that we learned about it on CTV, not during the many hours of meetings we had just had with our Liberal partners.

I checked with Layton's team to see if he or they had agreed to this panel. No one on our team had heard of it before.

I called Romanow to ask what he knew about it. He reported that he had heard about this committee from a *Globe and Mail* journalist who had just called to ask for comment. He had not been approached by anyone from the Liberals or the NDP. Seizing opportunity (our theme that weekend), I asked Romanow if he would be willing to serve on such a panel, and he said he would.

A little later in the proceedings, I asked Herb Metcalfe what was up with this panel, and gently reminded him of our "no surprises" clause. I asked him if Martin, McKenna, and Manley had agreed to serve on it, and reported to him that Romanow seemed willing to do so. Metcalfe said a string of words that were hard to follow, on the theme of "let's talk about this later."

As far as I can make out, this was another attempt by Dion and his team to reassure their party that plague, earthquakes, and widespread volcanoes were not going to be visited on Canada as a result of the new government. The candidates for the proposed committee mostly maintained a dignified silence about it until it became moot.

It's odd, in hindsight, how we drifted into that afternoon's press conference without any discussion or debate about its form, purpose, or strategy. None of the Liberal staff ever seemed to sleep. They weren't talking to us much that afternoon. The Bloc didn't care how the coalition was communicated to English Canada, and knew it was already selling well in the French-language press. And we—I—decided to be deferential.

Mr. Dion's team seemed to be extremely sensitive about their prerogatives, and very quick to take responsibility for documents and logistics ("always grab the typewriter" is an excellent strategy in many situations). The Liberal team overall had made huge play about the fact that the new government would be *led* by the Liberal Party. It was to be the *Liberal-led* "co-operative" government, not a "coalition" government, a word they seemed to want to banish from the language. The optics of being in total control of everything seemed to be critical to holding the Liberal team together on the accords.

It seemed sensible to me, in turn, to play along with this to get the agreement done—perhaps an example of the cat resting satisfied with its canary before it has really swallowed it.

At about 3:00 p.m., Dion, Layton, and Duceppe met in Dion's office. The Liberal staff had prepared numerous copies of the agreements in French and English, and these were signed by the three leaders. They stood for a group photo with their senior political staff while a few of us lurked off-camera. (I was checking out the beautiful Edwardian murals in Dion's office, which had traditionally been the Prime Minister's Office, until Diefenbaker refused to leave it.)

At one point in the proceedings, Mr. Duceppe, a very able parliamentarian and politician, gently warned the Liberal staff in an aside (but in my hearing) to be careful how they staged things that day, given that the Bloc Québécois's role might be controversial in English Canada.

This had no effect on arrangements.

Then we all trooped off for a joint press conference to do a for-show signing in front of the media, to make statements, and to answer questions.

It took a few hours for Prime Minister Harper's staff to figure it out, but they quickly twigged to the gift we gave them during that press conference. Dion, Layton, and Duceppe "signed" a piece of paper together. They sat together. They made statements together. They answered questions together. To any reasonable person, it looked as if the three parties were all going into government together. This was not the case. The Liberals and NDP were going into office together, and the Bloc was agreeing to support the new government in the House of Commons for its first budget, with all bets off after that.

But that was the prose. The poetry was that the Liberal Party of Canada and the New Democratic Party of Canada were "gonna run the government with separatists"—just as my friend from Mr. Harper's circle had put it to me a few days before. No amount of explaining could erase the television image. And as political veterans from the Saskatchewan

NDP have been telling young aspirants for many generations, "when you're explaining, you're losing."

Mr. Dion should have held a press conference by himself, perhaps with the three Liberal-leadership candidates by his side, to announce that he had succeeded in reaching an agreement with a majority of the MPs in Parliament to form a new government. Layton could then have commented separately. In light of how things spun in English Canada, it would have been wise for Gilles Duceppe to reserve comment for a day or two, so that he could have stayed out of the visual.

This wasn't a federal-provincial meeting; those weren't intergovernmental accords; it didn't make sense to stage the event as a first ministers' meeting. I didn't understand any of this at the time, alas. I was used to first ministers' meetings from my time working for Premier Romanow. It all seemed normal to me.

That press conference was, basically, the last time the coalition partners were in control of events. In many ways this story ends here, in a fundamental failure by our entire team in all its bits and pieces to understand that, once the accords were negotiated, our work had only begun. As a political proposition, the coalition essentially died during its very first step out of the gate. Everything else was end-game.

At 8:45 p.m. that night I received an e-mail from Paul Zed, from Michael Ignatieff's campaign: "You pulled it off. Congrats, well done."

That's the way it looked, for one more day.

Tuesday, December 2, 2008

THINGS WENT VERY BADLY.

The prime minister and the Conservative anger machine zeroed in on the key weakness of the coalition project, the high-profile role of the Bloc Québécois. In a high-decibel question period, Mr. Harper staked out the blue team's counter-attack. This exchange, which led question period on Tuesday December 2, set the tone:

> *Hon. Stéphane Dion: Mr. Speaker, I will read the following statement: "The whole principle of our democracy is the government is supposed to be able to face the House of Commons any day on a vote. This government now has a deliberate policy of avoiding a vote . . . " The statement goes on to say that it is a violation of the fundamental constitutional principles of our democracy. Could the prime minister inform the house who said those words?*
>
> *Right Hon. Stephen Harper: Mr. Speaker, the highest principle of Canadian democracy is that if one wants to be Prime Minister one gets one's mandate from the Canadian people and not from Quebec*

separatists. The deal that the leader of the Liberal Party has made with the separatists is a betrayal of the voters of this country, a betrayal of the best interests of our economy, and a betrayal of the best interests of our country, and we will fight it with every means that we have.

Hon. Stéphane Dion: Mr. Speaker, the Prime Minister did not answer my question. I will help him. He himself spoke those words on May 3, 2005, when he was the leader of the Opposition. Let me repeat what the Prime Minister said: "This government now has the deliberate policy of avoiding a vote. This is a violation of the fundamental constitutional principles of our democracy." Does the Prime Minister agree with himself?

Right Hon. Stephen Harper: Mr. Speaker, as I have just said, if one wants to be Prime Minister one gets one's mandate from the Canadian people and not from Quebec separatists. From Macdonald and Laurier to Diefenbaker and Trudeau, Liberals and Conservatives have often disagreed, but there is one thing we should never disagree on and the leader of the Liberal Party is betraying the best interests in the best traditions of his own party if he thinks he can make a deal to govern.

Hon. Stéphane Dion: Mr. Speaker, every member of the house has received a mandate from the Canadian people to deliver a government that will face the economic crisis. The Prime Minister has failed. The Prime Minister does not have the support of the house any more. Will he allow a vote to test if he has the confidence of the house, as it must be in a parliamentary democracy?

Right Hon. Stephen Harper: Mr. Speaker, not a single member of the house, not even a member of the Bloc, received a mandate to have a government in which the separatists would be part of the coalition. If the Leader of the Opposition thinks he has support for this, he should have the confidence to take this to the people of Canada who will reject it.

Mr. Dion reads a good deal better on paper than he sounded on television that day, a fact that was about to destroy him.

In his exchanges with the prime minister, he cogently pointed out that the prime minister was flouting the fundamental principles of responsible government, and was behaving in the manner of a hypocrite, having argued the opposite case on all the issues in the recent past.

The prime minister's very first line captured the whole Conservative case: "Mr. Speaker, the highest principle of Canadian democracy is that if one wants to be Prime Minister one gets one's mandate from the Canadian people and not from Quebec separatists."

That, of course, is not true. The highest principle of Canadian democracy is that *Parliament* gets its mandate from the Canadian people, and then selects a ministry from among its ranks to do its bidding. But truth had nothing to do with what happened next.

If the shoe had been on the other foot, and it had been Stephen Harper's Conservatives at the head of a parliamentary majority making a move in the first days of a new Parliament to unseat an isolated minority government (as Mr. Harper had been planning to do when he was an Opposition leader), English-speaking Canadians on December 2 and 3, 2008, would have heard a very different song from their television networks, open-mouth radio, newspapers, and magazines. They would have been listening to lectures about parliamentary history, parliamentary democracy, responsible government, the need for the executive to be democratically accountable—and the need for the executive to find its legitimacy from a majority of the House of Commons each and every day of its existence, failing which the house had both the power and the duty to install a new ministry that could command that support.

But in this case, it was an isolated minority Conservative government that had lost its parliamentary support. And so it was the Conservative prime minister's themes that English Canadians heard.

As became immediately clear, Stéphane Dion had no hope of making his own case over the combined efforts of the prime minister, the Conservative Party's anger machine (reflected in hundreds of staff-generated "reader" posts on media Internet sites, and in many other ways), and conservative pundits. Dion was in a fixed poker game, just as he had been in Quebec during his stint as intergovernmental affairs minister. This time, he had his home province with him. The rest of the country was his problem. He needed to kick over the table. He needed to do something audacious and game-changing, in the style of his *Clarity Act* initiatives. He needed to find a way to speak directly to the people of Canada, and compellingly persuade them that, notwithstanding most of what they were allowed to hear about what was happening in Ottawa, Parliament was in fact moving to give them the better, smarter, progressive government that 62 per cent of them had voted for.

As Pierre Trudeau would have put it, Dion needed to go over the heads of the elites and take his case directly to the people. An opportunity would emerge to do this the following day. An opportunity that, as things developed, was going to come only once.

Wednesday,
December 3, 2008

THERE WAS A BIT OF THE FLAVOUR OF A PHONY WAR on December 3 on Parliament Hill.

From the perspective of the New Democrat team, it was an oddly quiet day. Our Liberal partners were preoccupied with talking to themselves, and dripped out information with a dropper. By noon, we knew two things: the three coalition partners were going to try to co-ordinate their work in question period to avoid the devastating pounding inflicted on us by the prime minister the previous day. The Liberals also disclosed, in fragments over the course of the day, that agreement had been reached with the television networks to broadcast statements by the prime minister and Mr. Dion to the Canadian people that night.

Neither Mr. Layton nor Mr. Duceppe would be included in these broadcasts, although the cable news outlets eventually agreed to carry them after Harper and Dion had spoken. We learned that both Harper and Dion would be preparing pre-recorded broadcasts. The Liberals let us know they didn't need any help to do theirs, and encouraged us to simply be supportive of Mr. Dion after he had spoken. They then hunkered down in their offices to prepare for question period and their statement.

Our communications team talked about what to do. We didn't like being locked out of the main broadcast, but there was nothing we could do about it. We would just have to hope that Layton's statement would get clipped into the evening news that night (as it was—although by then it didn't matter). We agreed we weren't interested in pre-recording a statement, since we wanted to know what Harper and Dion were going to say before responding.

Further, our team, fresh off an excellently staged election campaign, liked the idea of putting Layton in front of the doors of the House of Commons to emphasize that the prime minister was probably about to padlock them. (Those of us who dote on Saskatchewan political history recalled that Liberal leader Ross Thatcher did precisely the same thing to excellent effect during a dispute with the CCF government in the early 1960s. Famously, in Saskatchewan, Thatcher kicked the door to the legislative chamber to symbolize that the government had locked it.) Finally, by making a statement in the lobby of the House of Commons, we could rely on the parliamentary press gallery to worry about the lights and the camera work, broadcasting seamlessly using the facilities available to them on Parliament Hill.

Question period was noisy but irrelevant. Everyone was waiting to see what Harper and Dion would say to the public in their unmediated moments on national television that night.

Late in the day, my BlackBerry buzzed and I read the following from the Prime Minister's Office. It had found its way to me after numerous forwards and devious "bcc"s:

The PM will address the nation tonight at 7:00 p.m. He will speak for about ten minutes. Negotiations are ongoing, but it appears that the coalition will be represented by one speaker to respond to the PM, namely Mr. Dion. (One network said it was not interested in presenting a "yard sale" of leaders, and it was not CTV that said that.) While the PM's remarks are not yet final, he will make the following points:

- Canada has a rich history of democracy, the foundation of which is government chosen by the people;

- These rich democratic roots have made us the envy of the world and enabled us to welcome millions from around the world;

- A few weeks ago as a result of a national election, our government was re-elected with a strengthened mandate;

- We have acted to address the challenges facing the Canadian economy: tax cuts, pensions, infrastructure, autos and mfg sector, etc.;

- And we will do more.

- I will meet with the Premiers on January 16 to seek their advice;

- On January 27 we will present a budget with additional measures to address the challenges facing the Canadian economy;

- In the meantime, the Minister of Finance will consult broadly with interest groups and Opposition parties to seek their advice;

- We invite Opposition parties to provide us with their views;

- In response to the steps we have taken, the Opposition parties have created a coalition that seeks to overturn the results of the recent election;

- They would give the separatists a veto over every piece of legislation and every dollar spent;

- We will continue to act in the interests of the Canadian nation, our democracy, and the national economy;

- We will take all necessary steps to prevent the coalition from taking office without the Canadian people having their say.

The Governor General arrives back in Canada late this afternoon. Early tomorrow morning, the PM will visit the Governor General with the request that everyone expects him to make. He then leaves Ottawa in late morning to attend an auto announcement in Ontario.

This was an interesting e-mail.

The casual contempt that television networks reserve for the political process and for elected party leaders (letting them speak to Canadians was a "yard sale") was absolutely infuriating, and helps explain the very modest sympathy that broadcasters, public and private, get from all political parties in Ottawa when they talk about their problems. It would also play to the benefit of Mr. Harper, since Mr. Dion was (as it turned out) the least effective Opposition leader that night.

The government's political strategy was clear in this memo: they were going to try to divert Opposition parties away from the issue of confidence, and into a discussion about what should be in the next federal budget. To create some time for this to occur, this memo confirmed, Harper intended to meet with the governor general the following morning to ask her to prorogue the house until late January.

Having the PM's blindingly predictable talking points helped Layton shape his remarks.

We provided this memo to the Liberals (tight to deadlines, unfortunately), but it didn't seem to do them much good.

With our own arrangements made and not really much else to do, the NDP caucus and many of its staff assembled in the NDP caucus room with some snacks, and settled down in front of a set of big-screen televisions to watch the statements by Harper and Dion. Shortly after 7:00 p.m., the networks cut to a video of Prime Minister Harper. His waxy smile and rigid posture clearly conveyed his nervousness. But he delivered the points set out in the PMO memo as predicted, clearly warming to his topic as he expressed his outrage—outrage!—that anyone would conspire with the Bloc Québécois to replace a sitting government, as he had done himself.

Our caucus booed the prime minister gamely, heckled his television image in fine House of Commons style, and waited for our guy, our nominee to replace Mr. Harper in the prime minister's chair, to destroy Harper and finally politically launch the new government. For a very brief moment, the NDP caucus was rooting for a Liberal leader.

No Canadian, with the possible exception of Pierre Trudeau, was less deserving of being accused of consorting with separatists than Stéphane Dion.

He had an opportunity here to make a devastating rebuttal to the prime minister, dedicated as Mr. Harper was to systematically dismantling Canada's national government with the parliamentary support of the Bloc at every step, co-author as Mr. Harper was of a "firewall" memorandum urging Alberta to partially withdraw from the federation, architect as Mr. Harper was of a similar coalition proposal he had been shopping only a few years before. Dion had the opportunity to point to the exciting new Obama administration just elected south of the border, to say that 62 per cent of Canadians had voted for identical change in Canada, and to say that the economy demanded that change.

Dion had the opportunity to point to the long winter of increasingly centralized and out-of-touch government in Ottawa, and to say that this was the start of a new era of responsive, accountable government, wherein the government, the cabinet, and the prime minister would actually enjoy the voting support of a clear majority of the Canadian people, and not simply be the lucky recipients of the undemocratic quirks of Canada's antiquated electoral system.

Dion said some of this, more or less.

But nobody who was watching heard any of it.

As Dion's chief of staff, Johanne Sénécal, wrote to me in a BlackBerry exchange a few minutes after Dion's broadcast: "It was a flop as to quality—I have no idea what happened. They tell me it had to do with compatibility of technologies. I have no idea but it did not look good."

I thumbed my own first reaction to Ray Guardia after Dion's video was finally, mercifully over: "Ouch!"

Guardia replied: "Brutal!"

My BlackBerry buzzed non-stop for more than twenty minutes as my various penpals let me know what they thought about what they had just seen.

A senior member of Ignatieff's leadership campaign offered the most ominous comment, a few minutes after Dion spoke (7:53 p.m.): "It's all over, Dude." I wrote back (7:58 p.m.): "How so?" He replied (8:03 p.m.): "The chief spokesman can't speak."

A few moments later, one of my friends from the Conservatives wrote to commiserate (8:00 p.m.): "Dion. You must really wish that Jack could speak instead of Dion."

I was looking morosely at the note from the Ignatieff campaign when this came across. In need of some levity just then, I decided to reply with a joke, alluding to some of our lines from the 2008 campaign, and then I added a little bait to see if he would tell me anything about the PM's plans for the governor general the following morning (8:03 p.m.): "Hey, as [Layton's] been saying for awhile, every time your guy quits, he's going to apply for the job. GG ruling is going to be quite something, one way or another."

To be provocative, I added (8:09 p.m.): "A little more seriously, that's a big decision there about the Quebec wing."

He mused about this for a few minutes and then replied (8:29 p.m.): "As you have been trying to tell your folks, you can't do good unless you're in power. So far you have played the Grits like a song. You know though, with every day, it's getting more difficult. Nonetheless, I give you credit. This was a big idea. I just don't think it will work." An elegantly written message confirming that Dion had just blown his brains out.

We then watched Layton deliver a compelling, eloquently delivered, well-lit, and well-recorded statement in front of the doors of Parliament to a small audience watching on cable news. Possibly a few more saw a few seconds of it on network news that night. But it didn't matter.

The atmosphere in the NDP caucus room was funereal.

For the most ridiculous of reasons—basic tradecraft issues of staging, lighting, and videography—our candidate for prime minister had thrown away his chance to reframe the debate and to counter

Mr. Harper and his force-amplifiers. We were not going to get to first base in the debate. And so Mr. Harper was going to be free to play hardball with parliamentary democracy the following morning.

We had one last card to play. If we could persuade the governor general not to give Mr. Harper a prorogation, then perhaps we could still take the Conservatives out, quickly and surgically. With luck, we could then knit together a better cabinet and budget and earn support over time as the process debate faded.

Another Conservative correspondent later told me that this was almost certainly a forlorn hope. The Conservatives had in their hands a manual drafted in the 1960s by the Privy Council Office, directing the governor general's work. That manual supposedly directs the governor general to grant a prorogation of the house to the prime minister, unconditionally and in every case.

My blue-team friend went on: "There is a big, but meaningless, debate in our circles about whether we should have let the vote happen. . . . No consensus, but one wonders whether: (a) all the Liberals would have actually voted for the coalition; (b) the GG would have allowed the coalition to govern (rumour has it she went to the Queen, who said that the days of "Royals" deciding who would form government is over, and the right decision was to turn the decision back to the people); (c) the coalition would have lasted had it formed government."

It's a pity the Conservatives didn't test those theories, really. But they didn't. And so we gave ourselves the task of trying to persuade the governor general that a solid majority of the House of Commons did indeed support replacing Mr. Harper's government with a new one—and that it was her duty to allow the house to consider the matter without interference from either the prime minister or herself.

Anne McGrath worked on this through much of December 3. She tried to persuade the governor general's staff to schedule a meeting between the governor general and Layton and the other coalition leaders, before she made any final decision on a prorogation.

The governor general's senior people seemed to consider this for a little while, but ultimately informed McGrath that it was not appropriate for Madame Jean to meet with anyone other than the prime minister. McGrath then asked whether the governor general would be prepared to consider any correspondence on the issues, and she was basically told that we were free to send whatever we wanted to the governor general.

Building on this thin reed, we communicated with the Liberals, reported all of these conversations, and suggested that all 163 Members of Parliament who supported the defeat of Mr. Harper and his replacement by the coalition, sign letters to the governor general to this effect, respectfully asking that she permit them to exercise their votes in Parliament as they had been elected to do. The Liberals pitched the Bloc Québécois on this idea. They agreed. Letters were drafted, and the tedious work of wrangling all the MPs in three caucuses to sign the letters began.

Thursday,
December 4, 2008

The Liberal leader's office had taken responsibility for all the logistics of delivering letters signed by the majority in the House of Commons telling the governor general they wanted a change of government. It was therefore strangely quiet once again in the NDP leader's office. We watched pictures of the door of Rideau Hall on CBC *Newsworld*. The prime minister entered.

We allowed our hopes to grow a little as his meeting with Her Excellency seemed to take a long time.

It started to snow.

And then the prime minister walked out, looked up at the sky to take in the Lord's judgment on his works, and announced that the governor general had done what she was told, and that Mr. Harper had been authorized to avoid a confidence vote by padlocking Parliament.

Speaking directly to Michael Ignatieff, Mr. Harper announced there would be a new budget at the end of January and invited Opposition parties to help draft it.

The governor general's office later told us that the petitions signed by the parliamentary majority didn't arrive at Rideau Hall before the meeting with Mr. Harper. A Conservative friend told me that, in their view, one way or another, the governor general is not authorized to "see" any correspondence from anyone but the prime minister, and in Canadian practice was barred from taking the views of the majority in the house into account in deciding whether or not to lock the doors of the people's house.

I wrote to Johanne Sénécal and asked her what she believed would happen now. "We continue the coalition and will put onus on government," she replied (12:21 p.m.). "So far we have not seen anything."

I didn't believe it. Given the response to Mr. Dion's video, it seemed likely to me that his party would quickly rid itself of him, and that the Liberals would take a much more skeptical approach to replacing the government.

We watched the statements by Dion, Layton, and Duceppe.

I wrote to the key players in the NDP election-planning committee (2:48 p.m.): "Seems more likely than not the Libs will now find a way to dismount. Hopefully in the process they'll give us the gift of an ugly dismount and votes to prop up Harper. We'll see what the Libs want to do to keep talking about coalition. Maybe a lot, maybe not much. So I guess our election prep discussion needs to resume."

Parliament collapsed like a balloon.

Bill Knight had been helping us think about the operating implications of the coalition, and he was a helpful guy to consult. Knight had been elected as a Saskatchewan NDP MP in the 1972 election, and served as our caucus whip during the 1972-1974 minority Parliament. He had then served as Allan Blakeney's principal secretary during the latter years of his premiership. Knight had then come to work for Ed Broadbent, first as chief of staff and then as the party's federal secretary and national campaign director. He was thus a principal architect of our 1988 victories. He had then joined the credit-union system, ultimately as president and CEO of the system's Canadian Central. Knight's next stop was the federal government, serving as consumer protection commissioner overseeing the banking industry. He now served on a collection of boards and worked on international contracts.

Off and on that week, I had spoken with Knight about some of the administrative and governmental implications of the coalition. He served as a "sherpa" into the topography of the federal public service, as well as providing us with much other helpful counsel. We compared notes on the talented tribe of senior public servants who have worked with NDP governments, and considered how some of them might contribute to this enterprise.

Now I needed one more service from him. I asked him if he'd come to Parliament Hill wearing his MP's pin, so we could hold a little wake in the parliamentary restaurant.

He indulged me.

We got a table in the main dining room, close to a group of Conservative senators who seemed for some reason to be having a party with CTV political correspondent Mike Duffy. We talked about the governor general's decision and what it meant.

"I hate losing," I said.

Later that day I thanked Layton's staff team for their work, packed my bags, and flew home.

Monday,
December 8, 2008

STÉPHANE DION RESIGNED, EFFECTIVE IMMEDIATELY. I wrote a last BlackBerry message to Johanne Sénécal (5:44 p.m.): "I'm sorry Mr. Dion ended up concluding he needed to step down. Thank you for the positive, open approach you took to bridging 70 years of history between our parties. Hopefully something good will still come if it."

She replied (8:31 p.m.): "Thank you. It was a pleasure doing business with you. It's not over yet. The coalition still exists. Wait for the next few days to roll out. Many people who support Michael Ignatieff truly believe in it. Next few weeks will be important."

"I'm pleased to hear that," I wrote. "As you can imagine it's a little distressing to listen to Messrs Herle *et al* suggesting otherwise [the 'openmouthosphere' was full of former Martin staffers urging the Liberals to withdraw from the coalition and to support Mr. Harper's government instead]. If you have any advice for us in the next few weeks please write!"

"Let the dust settle," she replied. "And talk later."

Tuesday,
December 9, 2008

I SENT A SIMILAR MESSAGE TO HERB METCALFE ON TUESDAY morning, thanking him for his friendly, thoughtful partnership in trying to engineer a better government.

"I haven't given up on it yet," he replied (5:45 p.m.).

"Neither have we," I said.

I decided to poke a little and see if Metcalfe could still serve as some sort of a channel to his party.

"Our leader has asked for a meeting with Mr. Ignatieff. Would be nice if those two could build some sort of relationship."

"I will be speaking to Don Guy [a key player in the Ignatieff campaign, and a well-respected Liberal strategist] on this issue and will get back to you," he replied.

We would later hear that Mr. Ignatieff had no immediate interest in meeting with Layton.

Wednesday, December 10, 2008

MICHAEL IGNATIEFF HELD HIS FIRST NEWS CONFERENCE AS interim Liberal leader. He announced that the Liberal Party was no longer necessarily committed to defeating the Harper government. Instead, he announced (in effect), the Liberals could now be bought. They would abandon the coalition and vote for Stephen Harper's January budget, provided that they liked what was in that budget. Mr. Ignatieff declined to spell out exactly what he was looking for. Basically, he invited the prime minister to guess what numbers he had in his head. He summarized his position by saying: "coalition if necessary, but not necessarily coalition." It was a paraphrase of Mackenzie King's waffle on conscription during the Second World War.

Ed Broadbent called me shortly after this news conference with some strongly worded advice. He said that Mr. Ignatieff had just explicitly broken the accord, and that we had to reconsider our position. I reported his view to Layton in writing (2:46 p.m.): "Ed doesn't like the Ignatieff messaging, and the idea that we have to wait until the end of January to find out if the Libs are in or out. He likes an early meeting with Ignatieff.

He suggests we give them a couple of weeks, looking for (a) a clear commitment to coalition; (b) Liberals sharing stages with us; and (c) (I would add) some serious joint prep work. Failing this he suggests we bail, blaming Ignatieff and going for the labour/NGO harvest."

I called Allan Blakeney and asked him what he believed we should do in light of the Liberal Party's repositioning under its new leader. Blakeney's view was that we should leave it to the Liberals to destroy the coalition project. He believed that Layton had a clear piece of ground— the New Democrats did not have confidence in Stephen Harper or his Conservative government—and that we should stick to it.

"We oppose the government," Blakeney said. "We believe the federal government must get to work to get the economy over the crisis, and we don't believe the Conservatives are the best people to do this."

If Ignatieff ultimately ended up supporting Mr. Harper, his government, and his policy, Blakeney believed we would have a credible position: "The Liberals have misjudged the depth of the crisis and the ability of Mr. Harper to get us out of it. If they fail, it's a Harper–Ignatieff crisis, and not a Harper crisis. If this doesn't work, Mr. Ignatieff must take responsibility for it. It's no good to say he'll wait. The time for action is now. He's happy with Mr. Harper, and we're not."

I reported this advice to Layton. Layton, his caucus colleagues, his staff, and his campaign volunteers would debate these issues for the next month.

What to do?

Broadbent's advice was a better fit for the way the parliamentary crisis was being discussed in the Eastern media, and for the way it was being assimilated by voters. Ignatieff had clearly detached himself from his own signature on the coalition documents, and was preparing to support the Harper government. There was good strategic sense in confirming this by asking Ignatieff for a meeting and challenging the Liberals to stand on some stages with us in favour of the coalition. Should the Ignatieff team refuse to do this, we had our answer on the coalition, and should re-assume our freedom of action.

As a strict piece of chess strategy, that is probably what we should have done on December 10.

However, Blakeney's view was a better fit for the way many New Democrats felt about things. They were extremely reluctant to follow Ignatieff's example. This was too abrupt a repositioning for the federal NDP, which generally tries to stick to its guns whatever the short-term reviews.

Having weighed his alternatives, Layton decided to work sincerely and steadily on the coalition through to the end of January, because he honestly believed it was the best option for Parliament and the country. If Ignatieff was going to switch horses and govern in tacit partnership with Stephen Harper, let him do so by himself—and accept the consequences.

I wrote to my contact in Ignatieff's team that afternoon (3:20 p.m.): "He's in! Interesting newser." He replied: "Thanks. Mackenzie King still has his uses."

"King was a crafty bugger to be sure," I wrote back. "I don't mind 'coalition if necessary, but not necessarily coalition' as much as some of my comrades because—lest we forget—King did ultimately bring in conscription."

My Liberal friend didn't respond to this.

January
2009

LAYTON AND IGNATIEFF FINALLY MET, on January 13.

Ignatieff told Layton he was worried about the legitimacy of a coalition government. He also noted that the Liberals and New Democrats had very different party traditions, and might not be able to work together amicably inside a government.

Layton tried to build trust between himself and the suspicious, conservative-minded new Liberal leader—who was about to make the first really important decision affecting other people he had ever made in his life. Layton introduced himself to Ignatieff, and told him about his extensive experience in government within the City of Toronto (which deploys a larger budget than many provinces) and at the national level as former president of the Federation of Municipalities. Layton argued that, if the Harper government was going to be defeated, it must be defeated now—a delay would increase the likelihood that the governor general would grant Harper an election, rather than calling on a new government.

The two leaders agreed that Ignatieff's principal secretary, Ian Davey, and Layton's chief of staff, Anne McGrath, would begin a series of regular meetings to keep communications open and to discuss the shape of a coalition government, should one come about.

I later heard through back channels that this meeting did little to lay to rest Ignatieff's concerns about the coalition project. Ignatieff was struck at how committed Layton was to replacing the Conservative government. He was suspicious of how a project to which an NDP leader could be so committed could possibly also be good for the Liberal Party.

Ignatieff also met in January with the executive of the Canadian Labour Congress.

Led by FTQ president Michel Arsenault, labour leaders urged Ignatieff to respect his signature and to work with the rest of the majority in Parliament to replace the Harper government.

Ignatieff, it would seem, attended other meetings that had a larger impact on his thinking. Writing in the *Toronto Star* in the spring of 2009, Linda McQuaig pointed out an interesting indiscretion on a tape, which was inadvertently left in a washroom by an aide to Conservative minister Lisa Raitt. On the tape, Raitt gossips with her assistant about a January 2009 meeting Ignatieff attended at the Canadian Council of Chief Executives. Raitt believed this roomful of captains of industry told Ignatieff that, if he persisted in attacking the Conservative government, his party would no longer be able to rely on support from corporate Canada. Ms. Raitt reportedly says on the tape: "They did it at the Canadian Council of [Chief] Executives, there were three presidents of major banks who stood up in the room—and this is not from cabinet so I can talk about it—stood up and said, 'Ignatieff, don't you even think about bringing us to an election. We don't need this. We have no interest in this. And we will never fund your party again.' "

Whether or not this actually occurred exactly as described by Ms. Raitt, it would seem that pressure from powerful groups against the coalition was brought to bear on Mr. Ignatieff, who himself was open to this pressure because of his own concerns.

Perhaps the dwindling number of voices in the labour movement who were partial to a closer relationship with the Liberals will note who got listened to—and who didn't get listened to—in this debate.

McGrath and Davey met several times in the weeks leading up to the January Conservative budget. Davey was frank with McGrath about the limited resources he could assign to work on the coalition project (the Liberal communications team had been replaced, unsurprisingly). They discussed building a joint communications team, when the Liberals were capable of contributing to it; tried to identify some Conservative MPs who might be persuaded to cross the floor and join a new government; thought about finding a new name for the coalition government, since the Conservatives had succeeded in turning "coalition" into a swear word; and discussed tinkering with the relative proportions of Liberals and New Democrats in the cabinet so that Ignatieff could feel he had improved the coalition agreement's terms in the Liberal Party's favour.

We were given to understand the Liberal caucus was deeply split on what to do, with perhaps a third in favour of replacing the Conservatives through the coalition, a third reserving, and a third proposing that the Liberals team up with Mr. Harper.

NDP finance critic Thomas Mulcair and Liberal finance critic John McCallum also stayed in touch. Mulcair was left with the impression from his talks with McCallum that the Liberals were still leaning towards replacing the Conservatives.

I flew to Ottawa the week of January 26 to join our team for budget week. On the evening of January 26, Anne McGrath and I had a last meeting with Ignatieff's team in the boardroom of the leader of the official Opposition. The team was represented by Ignatieff chief of staff Paul Zed and principal secretary Ian Davey.

My notes of this meeting, jotted down later that night, read:

Zed + Davey. Talked about how they will play budget this week.
We tried to get them to discuss (a) cabinet; (b) budget; (c) transition

arrangements. They replied they could not engage seriously until Ignatieff makes up his mind.

They probed us on whether we would consider an accord with no seats [in cabinet]. Also on whether we would do coalition without Layton in cabinet. They also floated idea of a "tweak" to accord to cabinet numbers to give Ignatieff an "optical win."

We replied (a) they are reopening the accord; (b) we understand why they need point; (c); we'll have a few ideas too; (d) Is there anything else?

Back and forth between Zed and I on political merits of the coalition. Davey supports. Zed opposes. Davey thinks [Liberal] caucus split 33/33/33. Zed says 50% are opposed.

- Not legitimate

- Tainted by Dion

- Bloc

- Polls

We gave them

- [Ignatieff would be] keeping Canada's [George] Bush [in office]

- Process doesn't last as a political issue

- Good government = support

- Not permanent with a minority

I didn't bother writing down that Paul Zed had not the slightest interest in a serious discussion with us. He ate up much of the meeting talking about his personal life. When we explained we were hoping to conduct some business, Zed became aggressive and dismissive. It was plain from what he was saying and from the expression on Ian Davey's face (which we had last seen on the faces of the Liberal negotiators while it was explained to us that caring for poor children is a fixed cost that must not be in the budget) that the new government was dead, and that Mr. Harper was going to sleep very well tomorrow night.

January 27, budget day, I called most of the friends who had been providing us with advice to ask them what note Layton should strike when Ignatieff reneged on his signature and voted to maintain Harper in office. Ed Broadbent, Allan Blakeney, Robin Sears, Bill Knight, Sue Milling, Roy Romanow, George Nakitsas, and several others all offered essentially the same advice: the tone to hit was regret, not anger. Mr. Ignatieff had just made an unfortunate decision that was going to leave the wrong government in office at the wrong time.

Layton and Ignatieff bumped into each other inside the Conservative government's budget lock-up (a room where Opposition MPs and staff get an early look at the budget, on condition they not leave until delivery of the speech). Ignatieff told Layton that, in light of what was in the document, the Liberals were going to consider a "strategy of amendment"—which didn't sound to us like "We're a team, let's defeat this and replace Mr. Harper's government."

When Layton returned to the office with this news, Anne McGrath sat down and took one last shot at trying to persuade the Liberals to reconsider. She BlackBerried Ian Davey (9:00 a.m.):

> *I have to say that I think this is unfolding in a very disappointing way. If the amendment isn't really really major (and unsupportable to the Conservatives) then we will have several more years of Harper conservatives operating as if they have a majority (once the constitutional window closes). The Bloc have been clear that they are willing to vote with the Opposition now but will have no interest in doing anything but sit on their hands and ride out this Parliament until the next Quebec election so there will be the instability of election brinkmanship with the Conservatives holding the cards and implementing their agenda. The sweater will be off as soon as the coalition threat is passed. I hope this has been thought through. If the amendment is something the Conservatives can accept then it probably isn't substantial enough and if it is something they can't accept then we still have a chance to change the political*

landscape. Certainly the reports indicate that the conditions will be accepted and I fear we will be back to the politics of mean. That's not good for the country.

Anne McGrath

Davey replied by proposing a meeting, which did not occur.

I went to go sit in the Opposition lobby to take in the atmosphere of the place. It was packed with MPs and political staff, with all eyes on the Liberals. Bob Rae walked past where I was sitting. Our eyes met, and he gave me a theatrical, Trudeauesque shrug—he had no idea what the Liberals were going to do.

The Conservatives presented their budget.

I left the Opposition lobby and went to the nearby elevator, heading for Layton's office. Ralph Goodale stepped in as well, looking extremely preoccupied. I said hello. He jumped when he recognized me, and would not meet my eye. "This is very tricky," he said. "We're going to have to do something very . . . very smart here." I wished him well as he exited and ran down the hallway to Ignatieff's office.

The following day, Mr. Ignatieff announced the Liberals would support the Harper government and its budget, for all practical purposes unconditionally.

Jack Layton patiently listened to advice on what to say in reply, and then faced the cameras and spoke from his heart in tones of disappointment and anger.

"You cannot do that and pretend to be the alternative to Mr. Harper," he said. "We have a new coalition on Parliament Hill. It's a coalition between Mr. Harper and Mr. Ignatieff."

The coalition Layton had hoped for—had thought through, researched, talked about in the 2008 campaign, and worked diligently to bring about starting on election night—was dead and buried.

Part Three
Postscript

Postscript

THE PARLIAMENTARY CRISIS IN NOVEMBER 2008 was a political showdown, an argument about policy, and a constitutional crisis.

It was about the fate of the political parties in the house, which continued to play out over the course of the following year. It was a struggle over the policies and priorities of the Government of Canada. And it was about the fundamental rules of the game in Parliament.

A political postscript

Let's begin with what is least important: the political implications and how they played out.

For the Conservative Party of Canada, the November events were a reminder that they did not yet have the power to undertake the kind of steps their team undertook during the early years of the Mike Harris regime in Ontario.

Lest we forget, Mr. Harris's first years in office as Conservative premier of Ontario (in 1995 and 1996) were characterized by an almost entirely unnecessary assault on basic public institutions in that province.

Notably, Mr. Harris and his colleagues launched a frontal assault on public education. And Mr. Harris set out to bankrupt the City of Toronto, downloading provincial public services onto that city's property tax base, an act of fiscal madness designed to cripple it financially.

After their electoral defeat in 2003, the core of Mr. Harris's team moved on to work with Mr. Harper and his federal party. It seems clear, judging from the package of measures the Harper government put to Parliament in November 2008, that they were once again in an apocalyptic mood, and hoped once again to overwhelm their opponents.

This time they wanted to bankrupt all of the competing political parties facing them in Parliament. And this time they had their eyes on the federal public service, including its feeble attempts to pay women fairly and the very modest bargaining power and labour rights it accorded to public servants.

What the events of November 2008 taught the Harper government is that a 143-seat minority was still a minority. The other parties in the house, even when lying on the mat immediately after being defeated in a federal election, had the tools they needed to resist such an agenda, and the potential to construct an alternative that could have replaced the Harper regime in a period of weeks.

In consequence, the Conservative government went into crisis-management mode, and wiggled out of the potentially fatal mistakes they had committed by deftly playing the governor general, English–Canadian opinion leaders, and, most importantly, the blue Liberal establishment centred in Toronto. How curious it is that Toronto's Liberal establishment, centre as it is of everything the Harris–Harperites loathe and want to destroy, was the Harper government's salvation.

Once Mr. Ignatieff was in place and had done what the Conservative government wanted him to do, Mr. Harper's government put their demons back in their boxes and returned to the incrementalism that had served Mr. Harper well in his first term.

It can therefore be said that the November 2008 events taught the

Harper government some important lessons about prudence and moderation, which it applied to its own benefit.

To sweeten the pie, in September 2009 the Conservatives were given a further boost, thanks to a second gift from Mr. Ignatieff and his team.

It is, to be honest, difficult from my perspective not to write ruefully about how the Liberal Party of Canada played its cards in these events. They negotiated an agreement with us. Their entire caucus approved and signed it. At worst we were four weeks away from replacing the Harper government and all it stands for. And then they reneged on it in return for nothing. Furthermore, they reneged on national television—with, shall we say, a minimum of courtesy.

Mr. Ignatieff dealt with his closest political friend and associate, Ian Davey, the same way. In October 2009, Mr. Davey learned that he had been fired when he saw it on television.

Mr. Ignatieff's caucus colleague, Ken Dryden, once wrote that professional hockey doesn't build character, it reveals it. Party leadership is like that too.

But to be fair, it must be acknowledged that Mr. Ignatieff and his political team were pursuing a coherent objective in doing what they did. As they explained to me on the first day, from their perspective the coalition initiative represented an unhelpful and risky distraction from a far-better-understood, less-revolutionary, and hopefully more-certain route to power. They wanted to win the leadership, raise some money, and then take on Harper in a general election the traditional way.

It was as simple as that.

And it wasn't a bad plan. But, as we told them, it depended on a series of things all going right, and that is always an uncertain business in politics.

Specifically, they were going to need the support of both the New Democrats and the Bloc Québécois to defeat the government in the house, since, contrary to Mr. Ignatieff's apparent view, he did not have the power to call a federal election by himself. The entire Ignatieff political "business case," their entire "plan A," pursued in lieu of the coalition initiative, turned on this point. When it was convenient for the Liberals to go to an election, they needed the support of the rest of the Opposition.

The folks they had reneged on—on national television.

For the New Democratic Party of Canada, these events were in essence pretty much what they appeared to be: a good attempt to rid the country of a Conservative government and to replace it with something better. Unfortunately, this initiative proved to be an idea a little before its time, and throughout the winter, spring, and summer of 2009, the NDP paid a price for it in the political culture.

Conventional wisdom had it that the New Democrats were sheltering in an unproductive blanket Opposition to the Harper government, were suffering a catastrophic collapse in their voting support, and had no further role to play. Federal politics was going to return to a binary blue-red pattern, rotating around Mr. Ignatieff's spring or fall 2009 election call.

The 2009 British Columbia and Nova Scotia campaigns provided the NDP with an opportunity to recharge its political batteries and to turn the page.

New Democrat leader Carole James earned 42.12 per cent of the vote in the May 12, 2009, BC election. Not quite enough to unseat Liberal Gordon Campbell, but enough to elect thirty-five NDP MLAs and to solidly position the NDP as the next BC government when Mr. Campbell and his Liberals fall, as fall they will. Our tribe was sorry we hadn't won, but encouraged by the progress we made in that campaign.

Then things got better.

On June 9, 2009, the NDP under Darrell Dexter won 45.36 per cent of the vote and thirty-one seats to form a majority government in Nova Scotia, defeating a Conservative minority government. In August the federal NDP held its convention in Halifax to celebrate that victory, and to talk about playing to win like that.

The basic theme of that convention—How shall we play to win?—was the topic of a great deal of conversation at the end of the summer within the NDP when it became clear that Michael Ignatieff had decided the time had come for him to call a federal election and pursue his own march to the Prime Minister's Office.

"Mr. Harper, your time is up," Mr. Ignatieff announced at a Liberal caucus retreat in Sudbury on September 2, 2009. The Liberal leader then announced, to paraphrase, that a federal election was now convenient for his party, and that Canadians were therefore going to be voting in another federal election, eleven months after the last one.

What to do?

Jack Layton undertook another of his meticulously careful consultations on this issue, discussing it with his caucus, party strategists, provincial colleagues, numerous allies, and stakeholders.

A number of points were evident:

Public-domain polling and the NDP's own research clearly showed that the public was overwhelmingly hostile to the idea of another federal election so soon after the last one. Was it really a good idea to defy the public on this issue?

There was certainly nothing in public-domain or the party's own polling to suggest that a reward awaited the NDP if it played along with Mr. Ignatieff. The Conservatives had held on to their support, in the range of 36 per cent to 38 per cent, throughout 2009. The NDP had also held on to its support, in the same 15-to-17-per-cent range (double the NDP's 1990s votes) we had seen going into the last election. The Liberals for their part had been slowly but steadily dropping since June 2009, and went into their September Sudbury caucus retreat on the brink of falling below 30 per cent in support.

What would be the point of spending some $30 million of our party's members' money, and some $300 million in public money, to return to the same Parliament?

There was a potential answer to that question. It was that, just possibly, holding a federal election would push a reset button, and give us another shot at unseating Prime Minister Harper through a new parliamentary combination immediately after another election. If this were possible, then the political alignment might actually play to the advantage of our party and our priorities. A bit of thought went into this.

However, on Friday, September 11, Mr. Ignatieff took that off the table.

"Let me be very clear," the Liberal leader told the media. "The Liberal Party would not agree to a coalition. We do not support a coalition today or tomorrow."

Just to make sure we got the message, he added: "I have a certain credibility on the coalition issue. I could be standing here as the prime minister of Canada, [but] I turned it down," he said.

Indeed.

And so, given that the Conservatives seemed in no danger of being defeated, that the Liberals appeared to be on track to repeat their October 2008 election debacle, that Mr. Ignatieff held to his views about "co-operative government," and that the NDP would likely return with the same caucus we already had, the New Democrats turned to considering their other options.

Perhaps Mr. Ignatieff had created a crisis, similar to the one Mr. Harper created in the spring of 2005. Perhaps it would permit the NDP to extract something important from the government. Layton investigated this at a meeting with Prime Minister Harper that did not go particularly well.

The next act, however, was a billion-dollar announcement by the government that it would extend employment insurance benefits for long-term workers to twenty weeks, meeting a long-standing NDP demand.

In the political circumstances, and mindful that this proposal spoke directly to income-security concerns among workers heavily represented in NDP ridings, Layton, his caucus, and his team announced they would not vote for any non-confidence motions before that reform was adopted.

And then Mr. Ignatieff moved in the house to force an election.

That effort failed, the NDP abstaining.

The English-Canadian media subjected Mr. Ignatieff to a merciless beating, proving once again that big moves that don't work can come at a heavy price. Both Mr. Ignatieff and his party were brutally punished in the polls, exploring the depths of the Liberal core vote last visited by Mr. Dion.

And so:

The Conservatives seemed to have smartened up, governing more prudently after their near-death experience.

The New Democrats got their game back over the course of the year, and notched some encouraging political and policy wins.

And Mr. Ignatieff's master plan—his team's step-by-step plan to engineer an election victory in the fall of 2009—foundered catastrophically, leaving him no further ahead than his predecessor.

This allowed us to say, with "a certain credibility," that perhaps Mr. Ignatieff should have tried being prime minister when the opportunity was there, since his own plan did not work out to his advantage—at least, not in 2009.

A public-policy postscript

The Conservatives smartened up and governed more prudently after these events. But that doesn't mean that they governed well or in the interests of Canada.

The November 2008 events were a political struggle between parties. But they were also an important showdown over the basic policies of the Government of Canada.

What kind of government were the Harper Conservatives delivering?

They were running a low-tax, high-spend fiscal policy—the familiar fiscal recklessness of Conservatives in office. They were throwing money at old infrastructure projects, while Canada's industrial and resource economies continued to collapse, our training and research and development deficits grew, and poverty and unemployment rose.

They were pursuing an environmental policy that appeared to have only one serious goal: to protect limitless development of the Alberta tar sands. In December 2009, Canadian delegates at the Copenhagen Summit on climate change got to experience an unusual emotion: shame for their country.

And the Conservatives were pursuing a foreign policy focused on warfare. In the fall of 2009, troubling revelations about the fate of enemy combatants in Afghanistan were being stonewalled by the government.

These fundamental misjudgements kept the Harper government on the wrong side of the majority of Canadians at the end of 2009—preventing the Conservatives from making real gains in most public-opinion polls. They hung on to the support they had had in the October 2008 election, but didn't seem able to build on it.

Going into 2010, it was quite conceivable that the Harper government's fiscal, economic, social, environmental, and foreign-policy failures would eventually overwhelm the Conservatives and create the conditions necessary to finally remove them from office.

With much damage done in the interim.

As Premier Romanow says in his foreword to this book, we'll never really know if the 2008 coalition government would have done better. But I submit that, in each of those areas, there was likely enough common ground between the Liberals under Mr. Dion (or a new leader from his party wing) and the New Democrats under Mr. Layton to reverse the Conservative government's priorities and to pursue better ones.

Canada can have smart, well-managed public services financed by a tax system in the mid-range of industrialized democracies.

Canada can better address its economic challenges.

Canada can pursue a responsible environmental policy.

Canada can behave honourably overseas and take responsibility for our mistakes.

Our country would have done better in all of these areas if the coalition government had gone ahead. That being so, from the perspective of public policy, the events of November 2008 were a lost opportunity for Canada.

A constitutional postscript

Finally, there are some lessons about our parliamentary system in the events of November 2008.

There are diverse of views in the academic and political worlds about what we learned about our system of government. Here is my view. The prime minister committed a gross act of disrespect towards the Canadian House of Commons on December 4, 2008.

The House of Commons is the only elected institution in Canada's federal government. Unlike the Senate, the governor general, or the prime minister and his retinue, the house is a democratic institution, our only federal democratic institution.

It was therefore entirely inappropriate, democratically illegitimate, and improper in 2008 for the prime minister to direct an appointed official, the governor general, to instruct the majority in the House of Commons on when it can sit or what business it can conduct, so that the prime minister could avoid a confidence vote.

The friends of the governor general's conduct will reply, fairly in the circumstances, that she must do as she is told by the prime minister.

The prime minister holds his office because he commands the support of the House of Commons. Harold Wilson, the former prime minister of Britain, had a great deal of experience in minority parliaments. In his book *The Governance of Britain,* he wrote: "The Prime Minister and his Cabinet are accountable to Parliament. They have no fixed term of office, such as that of an American president, who is secure for four years though perhaps legislatively impotent for part of that time. They survive as a government just as long—not a day longer—as they can count on the support of a majority of Parliament, however small that majority may be."

That is our system of government. The prime minister must respect it. And so, if it is true that the governor general must do the prime minister's bidding, then a heavy responsibility lies on the prime minister to tender "advice" to her that is appropriate, democratically legitimate, and proper.

What kind of government are we drifting into if the precedent set in the fall of 2008 is permitted to stand? A kind of plebiscitary Napoleonic system. At a time of his own choosing, our ruling Napoleon calls an election on such issues as he feels appropriate; the people vote. If a plurality gives the ruler their support, then the mandate of heaven is conferred and no one may question His acts until He is prepared to call an election again.

Ours would be an extreme form of what Quintin Hogg (Baron Hailsham, by then) famously called "elective dictatorship," the basic fault of the Westminster model when it is governed by an artificial majority engineered by the deficient first-past-the-post electoral system.

So what is to be done?

All proposals for fundamental institutional change—for example, replacing the governor general with a legitimate, accountable president elected by the House of Commons—founder on the impossibility of amending the current Canadian constitution without the consent of the provinces, who will want more power in the bargain. It therefore falls to the House of Commons to defend itself, as Canada's only national democratic body, within the current rules.

Here are two things I submit it could do:

First, the House of Commons could and should legislate to direct the prime minister never to provide advice to the governor general that interferes with the functioning of the house when a confidence motion is before it. This would hopefully make it more difficult for a prime minister to avoid democratic accountability to the House of Commons through a politically illegitimate and improper use of the royal prerogative.

Second, the House of Commons could (and I think should) legislate that confidence votes must come in one of two forms. Option A: the government is defeated and an election is called. Option B: the government is defeated and immediately replaced, at that moment, by a new one, specified by the House of Commons in its confidence vote—subject of course to final approval by Her Majesty, as represented by our governor general, who in these circumstances, one hopes, will be more attentive to the views of the House of Commons.

By making the intention and consequence of confidence votes explicitly clear like this, less room will be left for prime ministers and their ciphers to make mischief with the constitution or our democracy. The House of Commons can either dissolve itself and take its discontents to the electorate, or it can poleaxe the prime minister and his hand-picked cabinet and install another more to its liking—a constructive vote of non-confidence.

Lessons learned

The events of November 2008 taught us that the office of the governor general is no guarantee of our parliamentary democracy, and that the House of Commons urgently needs to take steps to defend its central role in our system of government.

What the events of November 2008 did *not* teach us is that the instrument of coalition government is undemocratic, illegitimate, or bad for the country. On the contrary, in a multi-party democracy, the instrument of coalition can do a great deal of good, as this proposed coalition would have done had it succeeded.

Here are four reasons why.

First, coalitions (if more effectively constructed than we were able to do) can provide the country with effective and stable government. Canadian minority governments have generally remained in power by giving as little offence as possible, by currying favour with Opposition parties case-by-case, and by bullying—daring the Opposition to trigger unpopular, frequent elections. Coalitions provide minority parliaments with a more effective way to conduct public business. They provide not only stability and the ability to take decisions, even if they are unpopular, but include the additional benefit of spreading responsibility for tough decisions among more parties.

Second, coalitions can build a government that a majority of Canadians actually voted for. As at this writing, there have been twenty-one federal elections in Canada since the end of the Second World War. Very few returned a majority government elected by a majority of the people of Canada (Louis St-Laurent, John Diefenbaker, and Brian Mulroney being the only leaders to lead their parties over the 50-per-cent mark). All other federal governments have been minorities, either phony, illegitimate parliamentary "majorities," elected by minorities of the electorate, or minority administrations pure and simple.

Mr. Harper argued during the 2008 events that he had a democratic mandate that the House of Commons had no right to challenge. In fact, his party received less than 40 per cent of the vote in the fall 2008 election, whereas the House of Commons as an institution received 100 per cent of the vote. It would be helpful if the executive better reflected that legitimacy, mostly absent in modern Canadian history. Coalitions, which can assemble a government that a majority of Canadians did vote for, can provide it.

Third, coalitions can help cure "elective dictatorship," by balancing the overweening power of modern prime ministers with government caucuses that have some bargaining power of their own.

One of the things we liked about the 2008 coalition accords is that we were going to be in a position to enforce them. This is a fundamental advantage of assuming a direct share of power in government. The crisis of hyper-centralization posed by "elective dictatorship" in the Westminster model is very real and is being increasingly widely discussed (among many others, by Donald Savoie here in Canada in a series of important books, notably *Governing from the Centre: The Concentration of Power in Canadian Politics*). Multi-party government, with empowered caucuses in a position to insist on a relatively open and inclusive discussion of major initiatives, can be a partial antidote to this crisis.

Finally, coalitions can be a good thing because they can be constructed to include parties that are successful in different parts of the country, thus reinforcing Canada's unity.

As I have alluded to above, after the 1980 federal election Pierre Trudeau asked for a meeting with Ed Broadbent. Trudeau discussed what occurred in his *Memoirs* (pp. 272–273):

> *I had a surprise for him. In an attempt to negotiate some sort of alliance with his party, I offered him and his colleagues some senior positions in our Cabinet. Even though we had a majority government, my reasoning was that strengthening the government's geographic representation would be very helpful in dealing with crucial national issues like energy and the constitution. We had a lot of members of Parliament from Newfoundland, Nova Scotia, New Brunswick, Prince Edward Island, Quebec, and Ontario. The NDP, on the other hand, had a lot of members from everywhere in the West but Alberta. I felt that the unity effort would be strengthened if we could consolidate our forces. There had been talks with the NDP along these lines on and off since Pearson's day, of varying degrees of seriousness. This offer was very serious. But Broadbent declined my offer, because he feared his party would lose its power and credibility....*
>
> *As I've said, I am not someone who spends much time pondering historical might-have-beens. But others may find it interesting to speculate how the experience of the last decade might have been different if in that secret meeting Ed Broadbent and I had achieved a common front of progressive forces in our country.*

Once the NDP was in a true balance-of-power position in November 2008, Broadbent helped to act on Trudeau's points. But by then, it turned out, Mr. Trudeau's party no longer accepted them.

The instrument of a coalition government may be a good thing in principle. But we made some important mistakes that should not be repeated. There is a little cottage industry on the Internet discussing this. Here is my take.

First, we did not take sufficient account of the fact that, in Canada, the prerogatives of the Crown have been assumed by our prime minister.

That being so, in hindsight the conversations between the Liberals and the NDP in November 2008 probably should have been conducted in the strictest secrecy. The majority in Parliament could then have misled the government into believing it would get away with its November economic statement. Mr. Harper and his team could have been sacked in a surprise confidence vote (as Joe Clark was sacked by the Trudeau Liberals in 1979). Stéphane Dion or his successor could then have asked for an opportunity to form a new government, knowing he already had one in his back pocket.

It is a sad reflection on our national democracy that there is no room for public debate in this basic exercise in responsible government. But that is the way Prime Minister Harper wants it, and, as we have discovered, the prime minister makes the rules in Canada, until the rules are rewritten by a Parliament that has decided to take back its democratic role from the dark corridors all around it.

Second, we placed a losing bet on the maelstrom of Liberal leadership politics and on the Liberal Party itself. As we discovered in Saskatchewan in 1999 (when the provincial Liberals imploded on the issue of being in coalition) and again in Ottawa in 2008, notwithstanding Pierre Trudeau's views, co-operation with other parties appears not to be part of the Liberal Party's DNA.

Circumstances may change this. But if so—and should our party again consider working with them (or any other party) in some sort of parliamentary combination—we must be sure there is a broad consensus in the other party's ranks before proceeding.

A future Canadian coalition government does not inevitably have to involve the New Democrats. Mr. Ignatieff and his wing of the Liberal Party, for example, might fit quite comfortably as partners in a future Harper government that is in a mood to continue to govern prudently and incrementally. I offer the same advice: make sure all parties associated with the new government are really committed to making it work.

Third, we did not take appropriate account of the political realities that attend trying to work with the Bloc Québécois at this moment in Canada's history.

It bears saying that many thoughtful, open-minded, interesting, and talented Québécois parliamentarians have served in the Canadian House of Commons under the banner of the Bloc Québécois since 1990. A number would have made outstanding federal cabinet ministers. Unfortunately, as these events have demonstrated, the nature of their party leaves them little scope to contribute actively and directly to federal governance. It is also true that these events reflect great discredit on Prime Minister Harper.

Mr. Harper and his party made a naked appeal to ethnic hatred among English Canadians to break the parliamentary majority ranged against him. In the process, the prime minister may have given the Bloc a further lease on life and stoked linguistic and communitarian hatred, dancing with the same demons that stalk multi-community failed states.

One of the actors in these events put it this way in a conversation about an earlier draft of these notes: "The objective of any government is to speak to overarching national purpose. Surely the most important is to maintain the unity of our country. When armed with the fact that the BQ is involved, what does a prime minister do? This prime minister proceeded to demonize the BQ for partisan purposes, at the expense of our unity. People outside of Quebec started to cheer him on. Mr. Harper's responsibility was to attack the coalition initiative without driving a bigger wedge between French and English Canada. It is the saddest dimension of this whole affair. It was politically smart. It was unquantifiably stupid for the national interest."

That said, in the circumstances before us today, a much more discreet, indirect, and prudent arrangement with the Bloc would have served us all infinitely better (including the Bloc, which I believe was sincere in its desire to help facilitate a better federal government). We handed Mr. Harper a sword, and he used it to damage the coalition, its component parties, our parliamentary democracy, the country, his government, his party, and himself. We should have protected Mr. Harper from himself.

Fourth, we committed numerous errors of execution and simple tradecraft.

There isn't a coalition school to go to, to learn how to explain and promote a complex parliamentary arrangement in the face of a raging attack. But that was nobody's problem but ours. This was our big idea. We should have thought through all of its implementation issues as well as its design issues, and we should have insisted on an equal role in executing them.

Among other blunders, the three-leader press conference on December 1 and the December 4 video were avoidable mistakes. We should have avoided them.

Fifth and finally, in hindsight, perhaps we should have dismounted from the coalition when Michael Ignatieff did, on December 10, 2008.

We had no heart to do so. Thousands of loyal supporters were just getting started on pro-coalition campaigning across the country. The Liberals were artfully misleading in their intentions. We had come close to pulling off an initiative we had been working on for four years, but our heads should have told us that the game was up and that nothing was going to be gained by playing along with the new, unhelpful leader of the Liberal Party. We ceded the initiative to an objective opponent, and that is never a wise thing to do.

We're just going to have to do better next time.

Whatever the short-term twists of federal politics, the New Democrats, I submit, have emerged from these events a better, stronger, and more credible political party.

There is a world of a difference between a party that believes in itself and one that does not. And whatever else can be said of the events I've described in this book, they demonstrate that the New Democrats are serious about themselves as a governing option—one of the necessary preliminaries to persuading a plurality of Canadians to trust the party with a bigger mandate and a larger role.

Further, where the New Democrats want to steer Canada is where Canadians want to go, one practical step at a time.

Away from the carefree fiscal irresponsibility of the political right, and towards prudent, incremental management of the public finance—the signature style of all well-led progressive governments.

Away from reckless and mindless tax giveaways to those who need them least, and towards a call to all citizens to contribute to the common good on the basis of their ability to pay.

Away from abandoning children as "fixed costs," and towards putting children and their families where they belong—first.

Away from the hollowing out of Canada's industrial, agricultural, and resource economies, and towards a prosperous, green market economy that serves Canadian working families as well as their bosses.

Away from creeping credit-card medicine, and towards better health care.

Away from a rip-off economy, and towards protecting consumers by cracking down hard on crooks, even if they work in office towers.

Away from heartlessly benign neglect, and towards helping families that are victims of these economic times.

Away from a grubby and snarling philistinism, and towards a fit place for art and for artists.

Away from contempt, and towards respect—for the people of Quebec, for the people of Canada's First Nations, for Canadians from diverse backgrounds and those living with disabilities. Towards respect for the excluded and the silent.

Away from the dismantlement of Canada and its federal institutions, and towards common goals that bring Canadians together.

Away from the dark corridors of executive autocracy, and towards the sunshine of an open, modern parliamentary democracy.

Making progress on these issues is work for a generation or more. But more and more Canadians, having drunk deep of the alternative during long years of red-blue conservative misrule, want to start.

So let's start.

Which is pretty much what Jack Layton said, to his great and lasting credit, in November 2008. And it is what he and his party will keep working for until we succeed.

Index